MODERN GLAMOUR

MODERN GLAMOUR

THE ART OF UNEXPECTED STYLE

KELLY WEARSTLER

with Jane Bogart

COLLINS | DESIGN

An Imprint of HarperCollinsPublishers

PHOTOGRAPHY CREDITS:

GREY CRAWFORD: ii, viii–ix, x, xiii, xiv–xv, xvi, xix, 5, 6–7, 8–9, 14–15, 17, 18–19, 25 (top left), 25 (bottom left), 25 (bottom right), 28–29, 30, 33, 35, 38, 41, 42, 44–45, 46, 47, 48–49, 50–51, 53, 54 (top left), 56–57, 58–59, 61, 65, 66–67, 73, 74, 77, 78 (top left), 78 (bottom left), 78 (bottom right), 80–81, 86–87, 94, 97, 98,102, 104, 107, 109, 112 (top left), 112 (bottom left) 112 (bottom right), 113 (top left), 113 (top right), 114, 115, 118–119, 120 (top left),120 (bottom right),121, 122,125, 126 (top left), 126 (bottom right), 131 (top right), 131 (bottom left), 131 (bottom right), 134–135, 136, 137, 140, 142–143, 150, 158, 163, 165 (top left),168, 171, 173, 180–181, 183, 184, 186–187, 190–191, 195, 198, 200–201, 204–205, 210–211, 213, 214, 219, 220–221, 226–227, 230, 232 (top), 233, 234–235, 236–237, 238, 240 ,241, 244–245, 247, 248, 249, 250, 251, 252, 253, 259, 260, 261, 262, 263, 264–265, 267, 268–269, 270, 271, 272, 273, 275, 276–277, 282.

MARK EDWARD HARRIS: i, iv, vi–vii, xxii, 12, 36, 55, 68, 71, 75, 79, 95, 100, 112 (top right), 113 (bottom left), 116–117, 120 (top right), 120 (bottom left), 126 (top right), 126 (bottom left), 127, 138, 144, 146,147, 160, 166, 169, 174–175, 192, 203, 206–207, 218, 224, 229, 242, 255, 256, 278.

JOHN COOLIDGE: v, xx, xxi, 2–3, 11, 20–21, 22, 24, 25 (top right), 31, 54 (top right), 78 (top right), 82–83, 84–85, 88–89, 91, 92, 99, 103, 110–111, 128, 130, 131 (top left), 176–177, 178–179, 188,194, 197, 208, 217, 222.

ANN SUMMA: 39, 54 (bottom left), 54 (bottom right), 64.

ALAN SHORTALL: 70, 189, 209.

TIM STREET-PORTER: 62–63, 113 (bottom right).

RAY KACHATORIAN: 185.

HarperCollins books may be purchased for
educational, business, or sales promotional use.
For information please write: Special Markets Department,
HarperCollins Publishers Inc.,
10 East 53rd Street, New York, NY 10022.

Design Concept by Susan Parr, ReVerb Los Angeles
with James W. Moore

Designed by Joel Avirom and Jason Snyder

Printed on acid-free paper

Library of Congress Cataloging-in-Publication Data has been applied for.

ISBN 0-06-039442-0

07 08 IM 10 9 8 7 6 5

CONTENTS

Words Cannot Express

To Judith Regan, for her vision and encouragement; the KWID staff past and present, for their dedication and enthusiasm: Sue Bae, Callan Childs, Tracy Fisher, Adam Goldstein, Sharon Gordon, Michelle Hanchaikul, April Harris, Edel Legaspi, Cristalle Linn, Molly Luetkemeyer, David McCauley, Frank X. Medrano, Derek Penfield, Sargent Pillsbury, Carolyn Thomas, Rey Viquez, Ellen Wakayama, and Marjan Yavari; my clients, for their inspiration and knowledge: Dean Adler, Judd Apatow, Craig and Kira Cooper, Bill and Caroline Douglas, Rob Dwek, Dr. Andrew Frankel, Nathalie and Todd Garner, Dr. Anthony Griffin, Allison Hamamura, Marcy Kaplan and Eric Gold, the Kor Hotel Group, Carolyn and Erwin Korzen, Mike Meadows, the Nazarian family, Tim Nett and Megan Derry, Billy Rose, the Rosen family, Mitch Smelkinson, Ben Stiller, Jeanne Tripplehorn, Leland Orser, Trina Turk, Randy Zisk, and Brian Zuckerman; all of the architects, landscape architects, contractors, subcontractors, and vendors who have collaborated with KWID, for their creative insight and wonderful work; the book's creative team, who helped realize and document KWID style: Jane Bogart, Jonn Coolige, Grey Crawford, Mark Edward Harris, Marian McEvoy, James W. Moore, and Susan Parr, with the contributions of Ray Kachatorian, Alan Shortall, Tim Street-Porter, and Ann Summa; my gracious design peers, for revealing (albeit unrevealed) meetings of the minds: Jonathan Adler, Simon Doonan, Miranda Morrison, and Kari Sigerson; everyone at Regan Books/HarperCollins, for support and expertise: Ginger Ahn, Lucy Albanese, Kurt Andrews, Brenden Hitt, Renee Iwaszkiewicz, Iris Richmond, Evan Schoninger, and Tom Wengelewski; the editors, writers, photographers, press contacts, and other media mavens who have believed in KWID over the years; my family, who supported The Bunny Shop: Don and Rita Dowling; Nancy, Wayne, and Tami Talley; and Mary and Terry Wearstler; my furry friends, for their unconditional love: Brea, Charlie, and Frank; and to the three hearts whose affection, devotion, and spirit have brought this book and much more to life, Brad, Oliver, and Elliott Korzen.

FOREWORD

Like many of the talented visual people I know, interior designer Kelly Wearstler probably could have been a really good art director, landscape designer, graphic artist, painter, movie director, or fashion designer. Like all visually creative people, Kelly's got a confident, curious eye, coupled with an ability to invent and bring seemingly disparate elements together. However, unlike most of the talented visual people I know, Kelly Wearstler could have also been a movie star. That's one of the unusual traits that differentiate Kelly from her peers: she has a deep personal relationship with glamour. Kelly's glamorousness informs every room she designs. And, just to add a little more to the mix, she's fearless.

In a tough, highly technical, and competitive field where the nuts and bolts of making rooms function is daunting, practicality often overshadows aesthetics. It's easier for a decorator to assemble a room in which everything matches than to concoct a space in which nothing matches but everything makes beautiful sense all together. I've seen thousands of seamless, tasteful, color-coordinated spaces that are undeniably comfortable and "of a piece," but they're also anonymous. They're faultless—and flat. In short, not a look to strive for. As an editor who tries to propose exciting and/or unusual options and alternatives for readers who want to live distinctively, I gravitate to rooms in the fast lane: rooms that thrill, seduce, and surprise. Rooms like the ones in this book.

In her early thirties, Kelly got to where she is because of her point of view ("let's make it special!"), an ability to translate fashion into interior design, and a talent for giving each room she tackles a delightfully eccentric or over-the-top focal point. There's a crisp and clean look to her rooms, and a distinctly playful streak allows her to mate fine, rare objects with "throw-away chic" finds. She breaks rules and makes new ones. "Status quo," "okay," and "discreet" are not on her radar.

You can't enter a Wearstler environment without being challenged to inspect, touch, and wonder where she came up with her ideas; there's an aura of adventure and discovery in Kelly's interiors. Not surprisingly, you will most likely feel dressed up and flattered—it's like the difference between wearing a tank top with Birkenstocks and a chiffon skirt with four-inch heels.

In order to do what she does, and to convince clients that they need an unusual, dramatic backdrop, Kelly's learned and developed the art of persuasion. You'll find it on every page of this book—page after page of clever furniture juxtapositions, luxurious materials, eccentric accessories, hand-painted walls and floors, and high-voltage contrasts of colors and patterns. You won't find a lot of "safe," but you won't find "weird" either.

Expect the unexpected: a typical atypical Wearstler roomscape pairs fluttery, kinetic chinoiserie motifs with slick, solid Samuel Marks furniture; eleventh-century Indian sculptures with contemporary ceramics; neoclassical patterns with mod-squad stuff; high with low; huge with tiny; sweet with tough.

From South Carolina to Southern California, Kelly understands the beauty of nature and man-made dramatic allure. From her big hotel suites to her tiny powder rooms, flattery will get you everywhere. If you're in a Wearstler room, you're definitely ready for your close-up.

Marian McEvoy

My Creative Journey

PORTRAIT

4

When was the last time an element of beauty and surprise captured your attention? Why does one seemingly common object make a glamorous statement, while a hundred supposedly special things just blend into the background? What, exactly, is unexpected style?

I'm always finding new ways to visually answer that question, and I can't recall a time in my life when that wasn't the case. Ever since I was a little girl in Garanimals (those mix-and-match apparel sets that teach kids to put together outfits that don't clash), I've been drawn to the visual excitement of the unusual and kaleidoscopic and have always found a way to channel that attraction into design. As a child, I'd spend weeks making special items to sell in my make-believe store, The Bunny Shop. In her wallet, my grandmother still carries a little laminated card I sold to my grandfather. It's sort of a dog tag that reads, "If I Get Lost, Please Return Me To" with a name and address line.

Because my mother is an interior designer, our Myrtle Beach home was constantly in a state of decorative metamorphosis, with paint, wallpaper, and furnishings rotating in and out of the house. When I left South Carolina to attend art school in Boston, things really got moving. The course work, international student body, great old museums and architecture—everything was different. It was a little intimidating at first, but I stuck with it and studied hard, waiting tables after school and returning to my studio space late at night to keep working.

By graduation I'd grown up a bit, and long since discovered that Garanimals are for the birds. I left conservative Massachusetts for New York City and postgraduate work at the School of Visual Arts. Between school, work, and an internship, it was even more intense than Boston. But it was worth it, if only to be part of a city that thrives on spontaneity and risk-taking.

In the mid-1990s, it was time for more change. I headed to Los Angeles to pursue a career in set design, and once again dove into the challenges of a new city. Ultimately, life on a film set wasn't for me. Besides being turned off by the egos and politics, I needed the stimulation of real-life needs and desires—not staged ones. Architectural and interior design became not just my way of creative expression, it became my way of life.

OVERLEAF **At work in the KWID bungalow, a 1920s Spanish house in Los Angeles.**

OPPOSITE **In the "quiet room" of the Spa at Estrella, a dreamy mélange of accessories reflects the Palm Springs resort's Hollywood Regency décor and mood.**

A supersized reproduction of an antique cameo, installed over the highly lacquered and elaborately paneled check-in desk at Viceroy, a Santa Monica hotel overlooking the Pacific Ocean.

The KWID Story

For the first year and a half after I launched my interior design firm, KWID (Kelly Wearstler Interior Design), the most unexpected thing about my work was getting a good night's sleep. Until I hired an assistant, I worked eighteen-hour days out of my apartment and schlepped all over town to pick up samples, meet painters, and handle administrative affairs. Over time, my firm grew to two people, then to five in my first Los Angeles studio, and finally to a houseful of employees, including architects, interior and graphic designers, draftspeople, an office manager, and several assistants.

Now that KWID is a multidisciplinary interior and architectural design firm, I have so many more opportunities to bring the unexpected into my creative work. With additional clients and projects, there's always more to learn and explore, and always a way to subvert what's come before. (I read an interview with a designer who remarked that he doesn't like clients who say yes to everything. Thank God none of my clients has green-lighted everything, either. Each forces me to approach every job individually, take on a direction I haven't gone in before, and work in different materials.) And with bigger projects, I literally have so much more room for surprises and drama.

My former Sycamore Avenue apartment in a historic Los Angeles apartment house was a personal laboratory for creating unexpected elegance: vintage screens that substitute for walls; layers of raw, sateen, and slub silks; majestic Asian art and graphics; and a backdrop of custom-mixed acid yellow paint.

Surprise Yourself

What can those surprises be in your own space?
They're really shaped by the individual and what he
or she enjoys—not based on regurgitated trends
that the masses have deemed acceptable or stylish.
Whether it's a gentle moment of humor, a design
element that catches you off guard, or a startling
shock, there's a spectrum of unanticipated elements
that adds sophistication and excitement inside and out.

Life is serious and hard, and you need to have
some unpredicted wonder around you to keep it
interesting. I hope that as you walk with me through
this series of KWID creative journeys, you're inspired to
reach into yourself and bring some unexpected style
to your own environments and experiences.

"Elements of beauty and surprise capture my attention."

**An ornate stationery set, sculptural ceramics, and a
mid-twentieth-century collaged oil painting rest above
a graceful cabriole-legged console and benches at
the Brentwood estate, a newly constructed family
home on vast grounds in Los Angeles.**

Seeing Geometrically and Organically

GRAPHICS

The word I use most often to describe how I see and compose is *graphic*. To most people, the term *graphic design* brings to mind the printed page: advertisements, typography, borders, and other printed elements. That's like mistaking a few trees for a forest. Really, graphics are visuals that convey something specific and are composed in a way that's definite and clear. Architecture can be graphic, as can landscapes. Good photography can be very graphic. So can fashion—my own wardrobe is proof of that.

Before I fine-tuned my interest in interiors, I got my feet wet apprenticing at two of the most influential design firms in the United States, if not the world. One of them, Milton Glaser, Inc., is best known for the iconic I♥NY logo; the other, Cambridge Seven Associates, is a multidisciplinary design firm that blends architecture, urban design, museum exhibitions, and graphic, interior, and industrial work. Both Glaser himself and Ivan Chermayeff, one of Cambridge Seven's principals, were strong visual thinkers. Their work in the 1960s and 1970s was very crisp, and though I was just a child during their most prolific years, it remains influential in KWID design today. Diana Vreeland, the famed editor of *Vogue* for so many years, also intrigues and inspires me. Her whole personal style was very graphic and distinct—an amazing color sense, those trademark glasses, razor-sharp haircuts, and of course a classic New York apartment designed by Billy Baldwin. I once read that she claimed "exaggeration is the only reality." Now that's bold and definite!

Whether it's an entire hotel or a single accessory, I want KWID designs to come across unmistakably and unexpectedly. The KWID motto is "the elegance of the unexpected," and it's sort of a measuring stick for the finished work. If I make a statement with a pattern, I don't want it to be simply "loud"; it needs to express a refined point of view. Black-and-white lines have graphic power on their own, but reworked as a houndstooth-plaid pillow, a geometric band on a curtain, or a zebra-skin rug, those same lines feel sophisticated and smart.

The bottom line? Graphic style isn't intended to be shocking or startling—it's design that lends itself to crispness and richness that make you say "Wow."

OVERLEAF **Carefully composed graphic grids in the women's powder room at the Viceroy. Crisp geometric treatments with vintage spirit–a checkerboard floor and ceramic tile laid subway-style–are softened by rounded reproduction pump faucets and the curves of Empire-period woodwork.**

OPPOSITE **A treatment room in the Spa at Estrella. The faux-molding wall graphics were created entirely with paint.**

Despite being described by many magazines as dizzyingly decadent, the Beverly Hills hotel Maison 140 is particularly balanced in its design. In a guest room, bands of molding anchor the symbol-imprinted wallpaper bordering and wrapping the ceiling, while the organic curves of an Asian ceramic lamp and European chair offset the clean-lined desk.

Shapes, Forms, and Other Simple Surprises

To see an environment graphically, you need to stop looking at a room as an assortment of furniture and accessories within a walled box, and start imagining it as space that uses specific figures and structures to make a particular statement. Seeing it that way is an intuitive process for me, but anyone willing to stretch their range of vision can perceive things graphically.

The world around us and the designs I interpret from it are bejeweled with shapes and forms. Some are geometric and mathematical, like circles, ovals, spirals, squares, rectangles, and triangles. Others are more organic, such as leaves, flowers, and other natural contours. Whether I use them two-dimensionally—for instance, as a carpet pattern or embroidered motif on a pillow—or as a three-dimensional mass for furniture, accessories, or large fixtures, I always seek out eye-catching materials and experiment with unorthodox applications.

It's easy to ignore the circle's power in design because it's so pure and basic; I think that's what makes it such an unanticipated motif. Unrolled, ironed flat, and reconfigured, that same little shape becomes lines and angles. These help make up the architectural and decorative bone structure of design, and without them my work would never stand up for itself.

Symbols that are man-made and naturally occurring are some of my favorite simple graphic gestures. When they're carefully placed—such as in an embroidered motif—small marks and logos can actually tell a complex story.

The guestroom onboard the *Kordura*, a luxury sportfishing yacht originally built by naval architect Edwin Monk. Seafaring symbols appear throughout my redesign, including nautical icons like a ship's wheel and natural ones, such as the sun.

Cabinet handles in the playroom bath at the Brentwood estate have a grade-school simplicity, though the chandelier and high-gloss cabinetry echo the sophisticated feel of the rest of the residence.

OPPOSITE At the Hollywood Boulevard residential compound, organic tabletop accessories soften a structurally composed, wall-side vignette.

Organic and unrestrained wallpaper
graphics surround tightly composed
furniture groupings in this guest
bedroom at the Brentwood estate.

OPPOSITE Whether isolated, repeating,
man-made, or organic, graphic
compositions and emblems have
become a KWID signature.

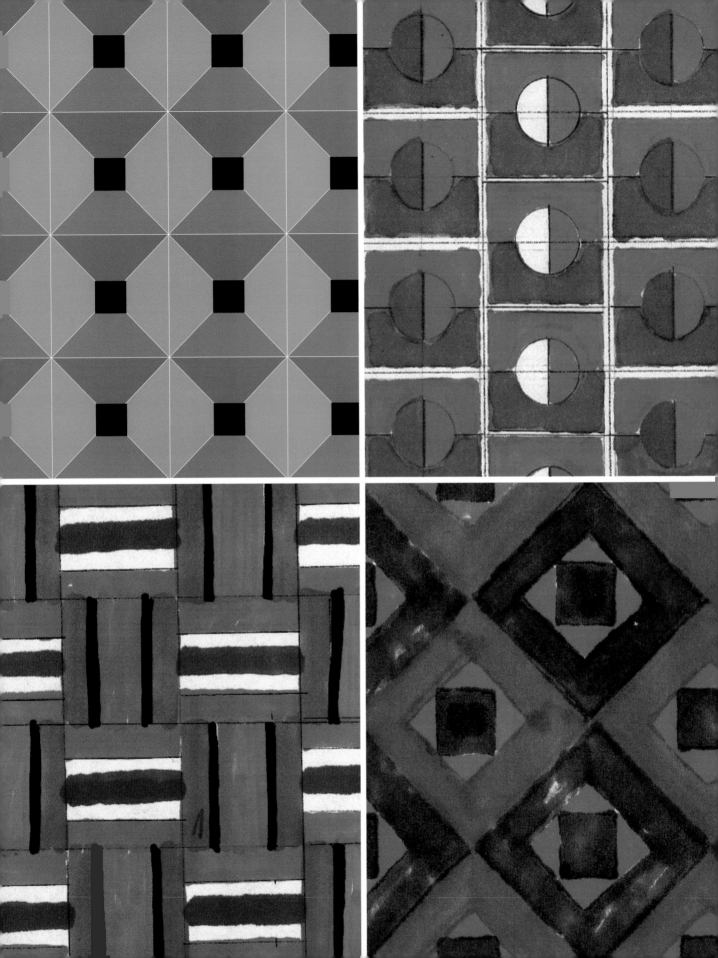

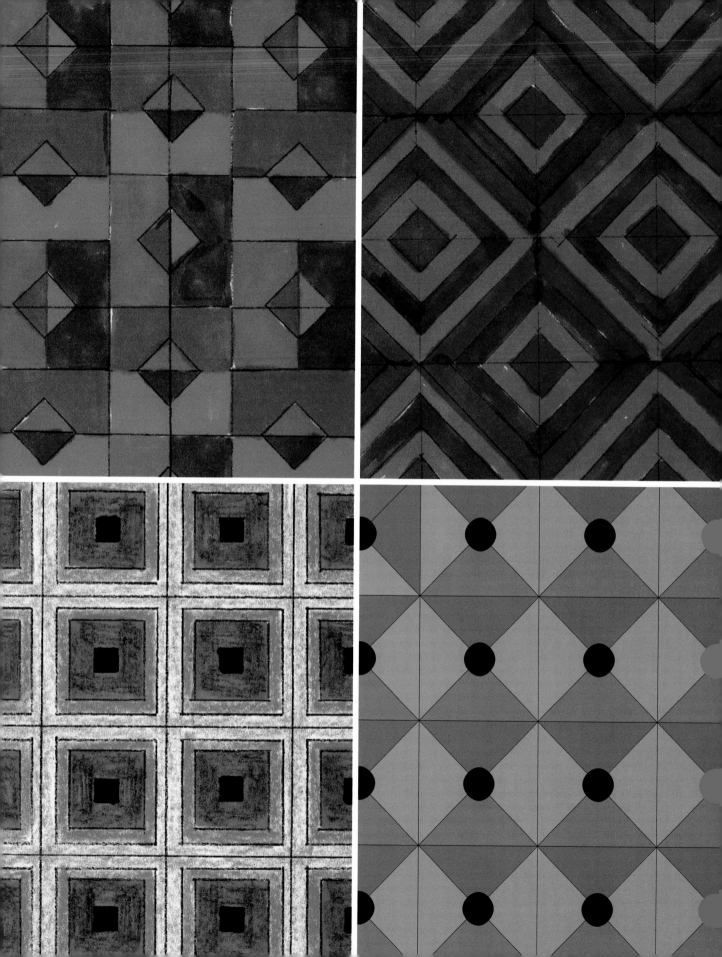

28

Orchestras for the Eye

KWID style combines, juxtaposes, and layers graphic elements as much as it isolates them. Bringing shapes and forms together requires compositional concepts such as unity and continuity. Again, I personally experience and explore these graphic design ideas without trying. They aren't rigid, external rules that the KWID team applies to a project on a spreadsheet or a proposal; they're natural criteria that are essential to a successful visual composition. Stopping to identify them—or discover that they are missing—is a big step in expanding your perspective on your own decor or design at large.

Throughout my work, I see a lot of unity and grouping. It's become a graphic hallmark that shows up in unique ways on every project I've done.

Besides turning shapes and forms into anchored graphics on which the eye zooms in, I also like to use them to suggest rhythm and motion. Detailed stripes and bands are vivid guides for the eye within a room and across space. They can be applied everywhere—from molding in a color that contrasts with its surroundings to a row of dangling beads on a window treatment.

Don't be discouraged if you can't apply miles of molding or don't want to roll out an elaborate, eye-leading area rug. You can add a simple stair runner atop an otherwise boring staircase. Try a flame-stitch or chevron-patterned fabric. Consider a wild paisley print that swishes and swims like a fish—it's a fun yet fashionable wallpaper choice for a child's room. The purpose of these kinds of graphic treatments is to keep your space, and your eyes, alive and kicking.

OVERLEAF **A series of Maison 140 carpet studies.**

OPPOSITE **In the Viceroy study, shelves constructed on the diagonal and filled with books laid in alternating directions creates movement in a room traditionally associated with stillness, while sets of chairs and candelabra converge in the study's seating areas.**

ABOVE **Loosely rhythmic, a chorus of glazed coral and ceramics enlivens a glass console in the KWID bungalow, while a duo of tortoise-patterned patent leather benches rest below.**

OPPOSITE **One of my favorite graphic tricks: grouping similar shapes. In the Brentwood estate dining hall, rounded vintage glass schoolroom light fixtures, an enormous oval mirror, and circular chair backs all seem to waltz in unison.**

"Crispness and richness that make you say Wow."

A Balanced Visual Diet

Bad design truly makes me nauseated. I stayed in one five-star hotel where I was so visually overloaded by large-scale cacti and desert paraphernalia that I had to do some visual housekeeping of my own (which included putting the comforter and some lamps in the closet). A lopsided composition or a theme that just doesn't end is not a very pleasant thing to look at; the same goes for an unbalanced room. My eye knows balance when it sees it.

Symmetry is graphic thinking at its most instinctual level. I begin to sense its presence when I first survey a new job site, work on schematic designs for a space, shop for materials, and install a finished room. Nine times out of ten, you don't get a space that's symmetrical. The architecture doesn't really allow it, so the design needs to make up for it.

Does this mean I avoid asymmetry? Hardly. Organic shapes and nongeometric forms are a real part of the world, and a design will feel too flat and dead without them. But I won't apply them in an unbalanced way—especially where accessories are concerned.

Scale goes hand in hand with balance. Never ignore the importance of it in design. A layout, an object, or a trim can all really influence your eye's initial "read" of your surroundings. Likewise, a room's dimensions, ceiling height, and other architectural factors can influence use of scale, but I don't let it restrict the dramatic expression for which rooms cry out. Sometimes an oversized element, if it's otherwise harmonious in a room, can be just the right emphasis piece.

OVERLEAF **Scale the heights: a broad band of stripes sweeps eyes upward, giving the ceiling illusory altitude in the Estrella spa.**

OPPOSITE **As cool and composed as the ceramic whippet at its door, this Estrella bungalow is a study in upright forms, sweeping scale, and purposeful symmetry.**

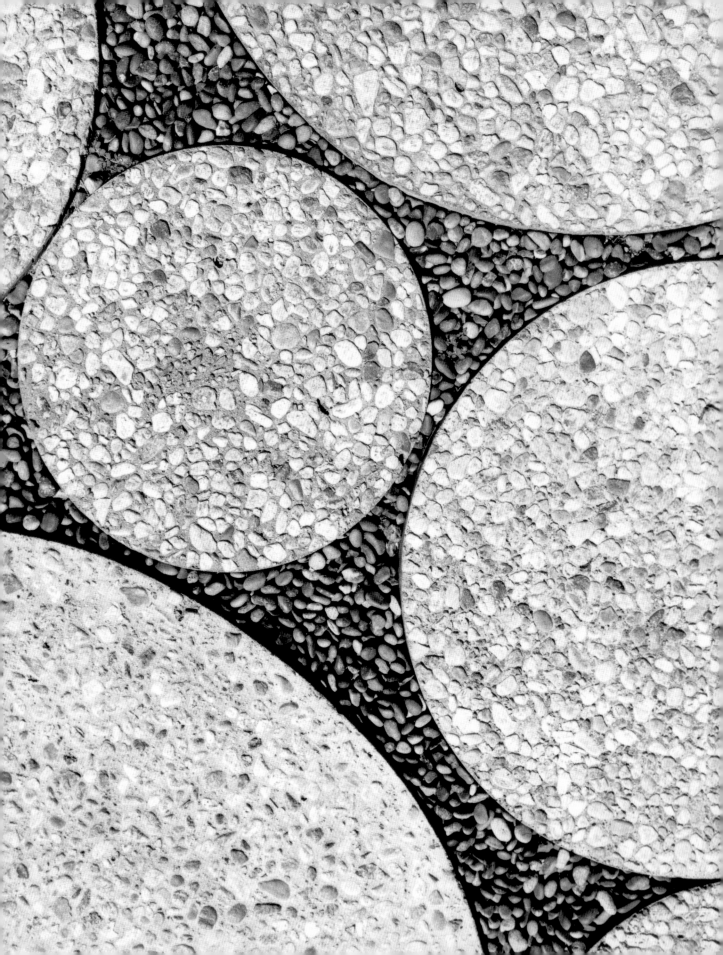

Space Shaping Space

ARCHITECTURE & LANDSCAPE

I always want to create a sense of place inside and outside a room. Places for living need to be very beautiful and thoughtfully designed but should also be those well-tended "somewheres" in which you want to work, entertain, or just hang out.

Making a stimulating sense of place starts with a space itself, including its physical architecture and the natural environment beyond. When we begin a new project, the KWID studio develops an interdisciplinary master plan for the property that synthesizes the client's needs, the architect's strategy, and, if there is a great indoor-outdoor site, the landscape architect's vision. This "big picture" lets me and my staff approach the property and its circulation as a cohesive and integrated experience, instead of a collection of design vignettes.

When did I start looking at a specific space as a whole? Probably before I could talk. But I became even more aware of the relationships between nature, architecture, interiors, and furnishings after discovering the famed architect and designer Warren Platner. Many of his designs—including the late, great Windows on the World restaurant—take advantage of the natural environment, frame and control the eye within a space, and use furnishings to build rooms within rooms. Platner coined the phrase "space shaping space," and I am truly inspired by his thinking. (Look closely and you'll see his awesome furniture line in many KWID designs.)

Landscaping is a particular discipline I've begun exploring more directly on my jobs. While I'm not a botanist or master gardener, I do know how intimately landscape interacts with interior design and architecture. On the inside, nature can be art framed by the windows; from the exterior, the placement and texture of flora can hint at the design that lives and breathes within its walls.

PREVIOUS SPREAD, LEFT **Bamboo poles dividing the adjacent lobby and restaurant areas at Avalon Hotel help define the interior space and unite it with the exterior landscape.**

PREVIOUS SPREAD, RIGHT **An iron bird holds the courtyard door for visitors to the KWID bungalow.**

OPPOSITE **At the Hollywood Boulevard compound, a 1920s Mediterranean-style property overlooking Los Angeles, we added a picture window to unite the dramatic local landscape with the interior.**

"I love to
be caught
unaware by
a stunning
surprise."

Divide and Conquer

44

When looking at and designing a space, I can always work with the existing floor plan. But since we work with the architecture, the interior, and the furnishings, I have to look at all of it to determine which elements work better than others. An architect is looking at the space and the hard lines, but I might say, "Well, I want to make a console, and that's going to be the division of my space." Basically, walls are just one indicator of layout and often prevent energy from flowing within an area. I frequently look to movable elements to make my space and the activity within it work more efficiently and harmoniously.

A rug can be the simplest possible option for space definition. On the other hand, made-to-measure screens and draperies can be more expensive and labor-intensive, but their price tags pale in comparison to the costs of "pulling permits" for construction. At Maison 140, which is inside a typically narrow 1930s Georgian-style town house, we weren't going to put in any walls to separate the lobby level's three zones (check-in, entry, and bar), but I effectively made separate areas with fabric dividers and a screen.

PREVIOUS SPREAD, LEFT **Inside out: Water-resistant vinyl chairs, Lucite tables, and British china bring interior formality onto an open-air patio at Viceroy.**

OPPOSITE **Octagonal porthole windows between the restaurant and bar at the Viceroy keep the energy flowing despite legal restrictions on liquor service.**

PREVIOUS SPREAD, LEFT **In the KWID bungalow, I embraced domestic conventions from the building's former life as a house. Instead of sealing the living room fireplace and hearth, I let it become the natural centerpiece for what is now our conference room. Its mirrored screen (another residential gesture) reflects additional seating space on the adjacent walls.**

PREVIOUS SPREAD, RIGHT **I commissioned artist Joshua Elias to paint a double-sided 3¹/₂-by-5-foot abstract oil painting to separate a breezeway from the intimate bar space at Viceroy. We hung it from the ceiling to keep the lobby open and flowing but still provide a spatial barrier.**

RIGHT **With its stepped wall forming a picture window on the nearby treetops, an Avalon Hotel patio functions as a living room, dining room, and private orchard.**

Southern California's natural light and balmy climate let me really turn yards and patios into year-round living spaces. At the Hollywood Boulevard compound, a fountain doubles as party seating.

52

Experiences au Naturel

Enjoying a sense of place shouldn't end when you go outside. Yards, patios, gazebos, and other exterior spots can host everyday activities and special events alike. This may not be possible (or desirable) in every office or residence, but if the opportunity is there, I want to make the most of it. I love to be caught unawares by a stunning view, tree, fountain, or other surprise when I explore nature. Instead of just buying off-the-floor patio furniture and rolling in Insta-Lawns, treat your own outdoor space as a special retreat or showplace—make it your favorite room of the house!

"I want to create a sense of place inside and outside a room."

OPPOSITE **In an Avalon Hotel cabana, interior elements (including a shag rug, wall mirror, and Achille Castiglioni's classic Arco floor lamp) hang out poolside with traditional exterior effects like all-weather fabric, candles, and creeping vines.**

FOLLOWING SPREAD, LEFT **In outdoor environments, potted accessories and hardscaping materials can be the equivalent of tabletop objects and patterned rugs that adorn an interior room. Urns and ceramic whippets trim an Estrella cabana (above left); pressed marbles and a spray of giant stepping stones carpet the grounds at the KWID bungalow (above right, below).**

FOLLOWING SPREAD, RIGHT **At Viceroy, I chose small succulents in ceramic cachepots to add easy-care greenery within the formal draped cabanas.**

56 The total experience of an environment should
encompass everything: the architecture, the grounds,
the interior, and the lighting, right down to the last detail.
Envisioning that adventure is especially important in
hotel design. At Estrella, I wasn't just using space to
shape space, I was using it to shape a whole experience.
Developed over a span of fifty years, the whole resort
was a tired mishmash of 1930s Spanish bungalows and
a 1970s motel that had been merged like stepchildren.
In coordination with the landscape architect, I unified
the property by treating most of the outdoor spaces like
traditional interior common areas.

OPPOSITE **To help dissolve
the boundaries between
indoor and outdoor living
in this Estrella dining room,
I chose silhouetted wallpaper
and covered every surface
with it. With the windows open
and the scent of citrus
blossoms on the breeze, it
feels like an outdoor bower.**

FOLLOWING SPREAD **The
redesigned and rechristened
Pavilion Court at Estrella.
Unifying separate areas built
in the 1930s, 1940s, and 1970s
was a real challenge.**

When guests check in and are
escorted to their rooms, they travel
along a pebbled path through the
property, as though the whole space
is the corridor. The topiary, busts, and
other garden treatments share the
neoclassical style of the interiors, and
on the three major lawns, there are
even more marvels, like a big tented
pavilion and an old-school game area
with shuffleboard and badminton.

"Design can bring the whole experience of a property together."

PREVIOUS SPREAD, RIGHT **Anyone can create an outdoor room. Cabanas may seem complex, but at the core, they're still four poles and some fabric.**

LEFT **A drop-dead gorgeous view of sky and land from one of the many patio and balcony spaces at the Hollywood Boulevard compound.**

OVERLEAF **With its arched entry, profusion of texture, and molding-bedecked gate, the KWID bungalow courtyard forecasts the experience inside the offices (left). Under a vine-covered arbor at the Hollywood Boulevard compound, my client can enjoy daytime shade; by night, it's a quiet nook for watching the city lights far below (right).**

The successful integration of interior,
architectural, and landscape design at Avalon.

The Power of Succulent Décor

COLOR & TEXTURE

Living without color is like living without love.

A lot of people don't want to do color because they think it will be dated too quickly. But color doesn't need to be short-lived. It's what you do with it, and put with it, that makes it work and adds longevity. I love to create communication between color and texture in interiors, whether in a short quip (like accessories) or an extended conversation (such as paint or wall covering). It's this interplay that makes a room inspire *oohs* instead of *zzzzzz*.

On residential jobs, one of the first questions we ask clients is which colors they prefer. Color should be personal to the individual who spends time in a space, with the hue itself selected with the designer's guidance. What soothes one person might ignite negative thoughts in someone else's mind. I designed one large house entirely without my favorite greens and yellows because the client felt the shades had negative energy. Hotels can be a lot more daring, and it's fun to use bold colors there, whether to suggest a historical time or place to visitors, to soothe them after a day of meetings, or just to encourage them not to take life too seriously.

Texture and color are like salt and pepper—they are pairs that make things much spicier. That's why KWID uses a lot of wallpaper, paneling, and architectural details. They make an instant and all-encompassing statement, often much more than paint does. Of course, mixing wallpaper and paint can bring together the best of both worlds. We often paint the ceiling and wallpaper the walls, or better yet, wallpaper the ceiling, wrap it down to a molding or chair rail, and then paint the wall down to the floor. My current favorite wallcoverings are reflective Mylar flocked with grit or fuzz that adds tactility to a surface across which you don't usually run your fingers!

At KWID, we spend a lot of time exploring hues, patterns, and textures, because they can be a clue or spark to a bigger design concept. When I hit upon a surface palette that's evocative, I build upon it with other design elements. For me, color and texture can be the most powerful elements in any interior but are always part of a composition. They can never carry the load for an unfinished design.

PREVIOUS SPREAD, LEFT **Layered wallpaper, marble, and carvings at the Green Bay Road penthouse in Chicago.**

PREVIOUS SPREAD, RIGHT **High shine, deep grain: A close look at the textural palette that drives the Viceroy study. Whether sonorous wood or glinting silk, the entire room is sheathed in these contrasting surfaces.**

OPPOSITE **Matte aubergine walls, nubby magenta raw silk, and a glossy wood tabletop in my former apartment on Sycamore Avenue in Los Angeles.**

Color Power

Where would we be without color in our world? I really can't imagine it. Color is so important in KWID design: it soothes, stimulates, and speaks to me. It can be historic (such as "royal" blue) or symbolic (there's a reason the term red-light district is used!), and of course, it can create a mood (do you "think pink" or have "the blues"?). Color can also reshape and highlight architecture and lend depth and excitement to a room.

I don't let fear of clashing colors scare me off. Most colors work together; it's getting the proper tone that makes them work or not. When I select a color palette or color way, I often start with one dominant color, then build on it with an analogous shade, or I vary it by using a different application, such as paint and fabric or tile and wallpaper. There's a richness and confidence to a room when it embraces one color and takes it all the way. In choosing a color value, I take into account the room's light sources at different times of day. A shade that looks aristocratic by firelight could feel totally crass in full afternoon sun, so we often apply it on-site and examine it over time.

"Living without color is like living without love."

PREVIOUS SPREAD **The lobby at Maison 140 forecasts the opulent overlay of colors and layers experienced throughout the hotel (left). A textural spectacle: toile background and sculptural foreground in a Maison 140 guest room (right).**

OPPOSITE **The entire Estrella resort is composed of tangy lemon yellow, high-gloss black, and cocktail-cool white. In the Spa, a chair upholstered in rubberized cotton takes on the sheen of patent leather, but resists oils, lotions, and water.**

PREVIOUS SPREAD **A thousand choices, a singular look: Using colors and textures in unanticipated ways can create a room's signature.**

LEFT **The ocean blue: To reflect the owner's love of tropical travel, we selected a resort-like palette for the lounging room at the Rising Glen residence in Los Angeles. The soft, aquatic shade extends across the grass-cloth wallcoverings, cotton window treatments, bouclé upholstery, and area rug; the bright yellow accents are carried through from an adjacent powder room.**

Patriotic and patrician, the red, white, and blue room in the Brentwood estate puts two strong primary colors together with a graphic flair. I didn't limit the colors to a single shade: the navy carpet sits under the postal blue chair, and the room's reds also vary.

Tequila sunset oranges, crisp
white cottons akin to sailcloth,
and glassy-smooth finishes:
No matter the port of call, the
Kordura makes a splash.

86

White is more than the absence of pigment: it's a complex and very nuanced tone. As anyone who has ever looked at paint chips knows, the right white is crucial but tough to choose. True white is almost never a good choice. It may seem like the prescription for a crisp and clean room, but once you see it applied and dry, it can feel antiseptic or shoddy. I prefer subtler whites with a touch of yellow, such as French white or antique white. They complement other colors better, are less shrill, and endure with grace.

Combining colors fearlessly has become another KWID trademark. I don't do it to be gimmicky or shocking; I just think that it's vital for creating contrast and affecting people physically. Transitioning from space to space should be an experience to savor, and I can make that work with a huge color change. Or if a client needs something more subdued—in, for example, a medical office—I use one color in varying hues across a whole job. And despite my aversion to rules about color, there is one I take to heart: too much color within a small space can be chaotic.

OPPOSITE **We transformed the whole feeling at Estrella with white paint. On the exterior, matte paint masks the frightening wedding-cake stucco. Inside, we hung lots of crisp white drapery to shade the windows, painted the Saltillo tiles shiny white, and added a snowy shag rug, another great texture.**

FOLLOWING SPREAD **Enveloped by a soft French white with taupe undertones, the master bedroom of the Brentwood estate is a study in warmth, even without hot accent colors. Oyster white silk and linen upholstery further complement this cultured pearl of a setting.**

"Texture and color are like salt and pepper—they add spice."

Texturize It

Texture isn't just a matter of flat or shiny and rough or smooth. Visual contrast provides surface surprises, and color lets me create it in a flash. Contrasting graphic elements can also lend a dimensional texture to a contained surface (fabric, for instance) or a bigger space (such as a room with a collection of varying forms).

I see layering as the essence of texture, and every surface deserves those layers. Wallcoverings, particularly when used with paint and moldings, produce an array of "skins" over a very large surface; when those overlays contrast, it creates a tension that's exciting and alive. Different varieties of wood—such as oak, cork, walnut, hemlock, birch, rosewood, zebrawood, myrtle, and ebony—all have diverse grains that produce texture at floor level and above. Sometimes that nap is stunning and I let it stand alone. Other times, I might pair it with a textural accomplice, like a woven textile or polished metal.

No matter how much texture I create for the naked eye, KWID designs also appeal to bare skin. There's nothing more luxurious than a set of high-thread-count sheets; when I travel to hotels that are being renovated, I take a set of Frette linens to make sure I get a good night's sleep. Underfoot, I love the feel of wool shag rugs and natural floor coverings, like sisal and sea grass, which also look so exotic and rich on walls.

PREVIOUS SPREAD, RIGHT **Lime green and golden yellow in an office? Absolutely. The lounge at the KWID bungalow. The stately dark wood floor adds a mature natural shade and texture to this brash palette.**

OPPOSITE **Layers of texture–from the bold basket-weave wallpaper and draperies to the lacy porcelain lamp bases–make the charcoal gray and white den at the Brentwood estate seem to hum.**

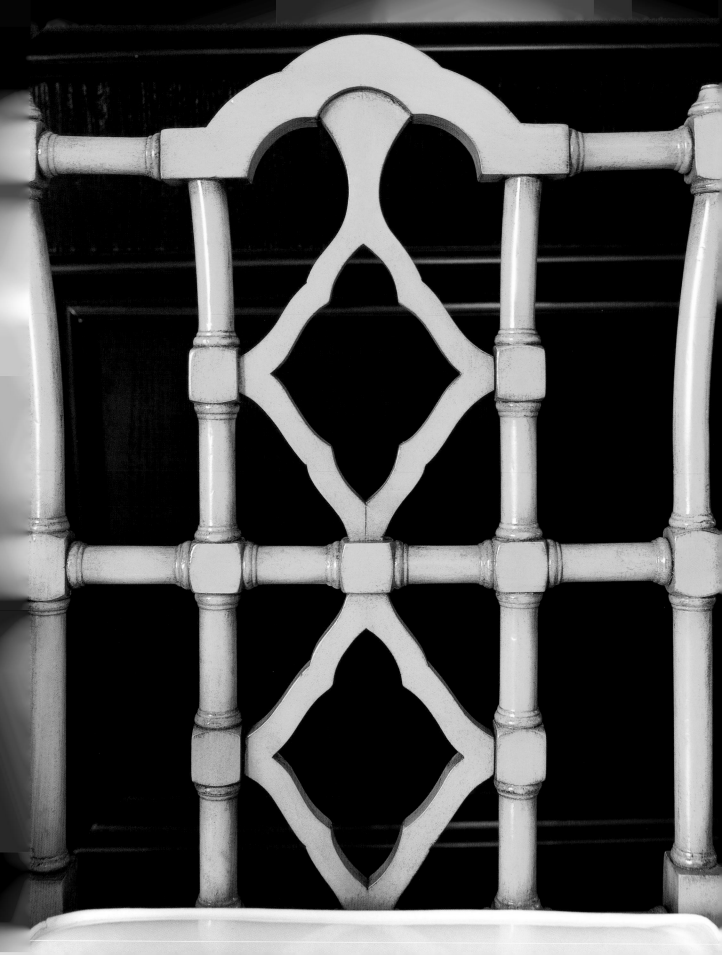

The Finish Line

There are a lot of conventions about the spatial effects of color and texture—like "warm colors and saturated ones advance, cool and muted ones recede," or "don't use a large wallpaper pattern in a small room." I never take them as hard-and-fast rules. Instead, I'm more concerned with the effect of finish. For instance, almost any space can look chic in dark tones, but there needs to be a reflective quality in the room, like Mylar wallpaper or semi to high-gloss accents instead of flat or eggshell. In very small rooms, the same holds true: light and shine vibrate the color and seem to make space expand.

If you are undertaking a bold color transformation in your own interior, keep one thing in mind: there's nothing worse than a bad paint job. If you want to paint the ceiling, feel free to go for gloss if the surface is perfect, but badly patched or scarred drywall and unacceptable prep work on trim are huge problems. If you choose a high-gloss paint, be sure to spray it on; using a brush will leave visible stroke marks. Hire the best painter you can afford, or paint as carefully as you can manage yourself!

Just as paint finish can determine whether an interior is successful or not, so can stain and polish on woods. While bleached "country style" pine is not my aesthetic, I do love limed and pickled treatments that draw out the grain, coupled with a stain that doesn't obscure but finishes nicely. On floors, a nice semigloss seal gives the floor a reflective quality and makes it shimmer; satin-finish wood floors feel too flat to catch light and the eye. Highly reflective lacquered wood is generally too impractical for high-traffic areas, but it can be gorgeous for case goods and paneling. For a blindingly glassy finish, I've used lacquer and even automotive paint. French polish, created by the application of ten coats of varnish, is the most amazing finish for wood cabinetry and furniture. The luster is unbelievably shiny and the depth is intense.

PREVIOUS SPREAD **Depth of field: At Viceroy, a carved wood chair hovers in front of molding and wallpaper (left); elaborate turned handles float atop a wooden armoire whose windows are lined with layers of French wire and fabric (right).**

OPPOSITE **In the sitting room of a one-bedroom suite at Viceroy, color-free reflective finishes contrast with rich matte fabrics. The gunmetal gray sofa, sunny yellow oil painting, and club chairs benefit from their light-dispersing backdrop, while the wallpaper would lose its appeal with too many other mirrored elements nearby.**

OPPOSITE **A high-gloss poppy color and reflective bedside pieces make this Maison 140 guest room space vibrate and transcend its intimate dimensions.**

ABOVE **Touches of luster—semigloss window moldings, ceramic tableware, a glass tabletop—amid broad matte fields (a sisal rug, wall- and ceiling-spanning wallpaper) catch the light and the eye in the KWID bungalow.**

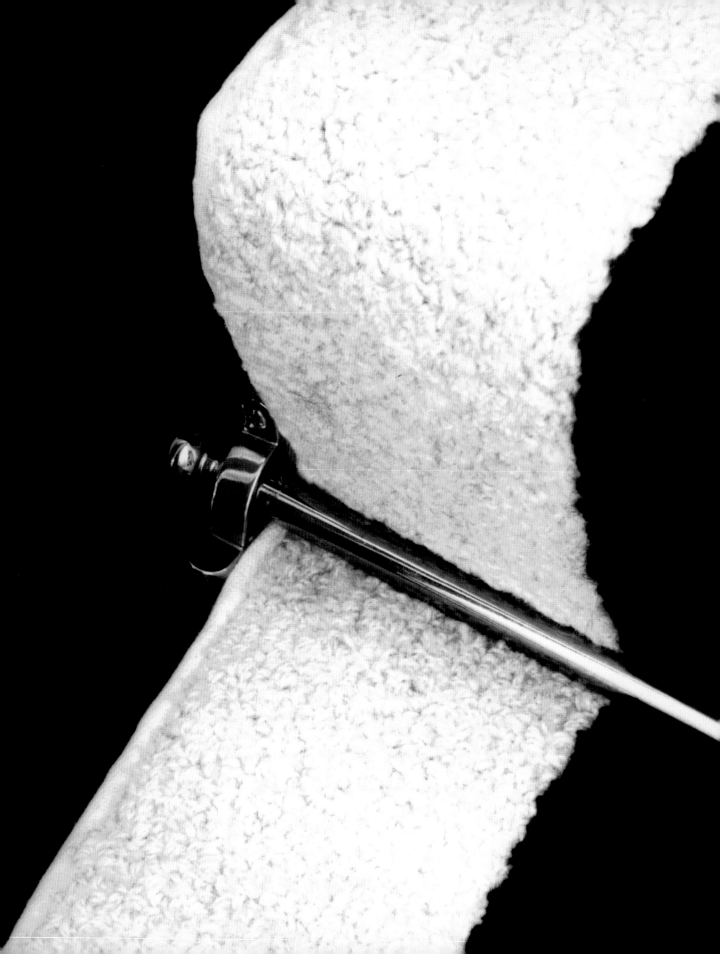

Embellishments & Accoutrements

DETAILS

The details in a design complete the story it tells.

These little specific fine points—a species of wood, the edge of a counter, the trim on a drapery, even simply a screw or a bolt—add so much to a design. Details add the layers, and layers add the interest.

If you ask most people what they consider decorating details, they'll probably mention things that are unnecessary or overly fancy. Actually, details are often functional tools that are taken for granted. Even in a simple room, it's the small particulars that make it look special instead of stripped. I'm so fascinated by details that I even want to see them in places where the naked eye usually never gazes. Suppose you accidentally drop your napkin under the table during a meal; while you're under there retrieving it, you should be able to look up to a great attention-grabbing dowel or beautiful surface, instead of an unfinished drop leaf webbed with dust (or worse!).

In the studio, the KWID team tests groups of details to see how they work together. We'll put a bit of oak flooring right next to a mirror to see how the grain looks when laid out at length. We take rug yarns and smush them together to see how a carpet we're designing might look once it's milled. I even cut fabric swatches up into really small sizes to see how the proportions of varying patterns and weaves look side by side.

Generally, I embellish upon and carry through the details of what I already have. If an interior is taking a particularly period feel, I might seek out accessories of a similar vintage to layer it further, or infuse totally unrelated items to bring some tension to the setting. But sometimes the opposite approach drives the process: One small item can give rise to a bigger story and really lead my imagination to a place where it wouldn't have wandered otherwise. If you have one treasured piece you can't part with or an architectural gadget that intrigues you, make it your starting point and expand upon it. No matter how insignificant that detail might seem, it could be the unexpected wonder that gives a room some spontaneous style.

Details are like the mouse that roared; without them, a room is a big yawn.

PREVIOUS SPREAD **Eye candy: an acanthus leaf pattern on a wingback chair at Viceroy (left), and a selection of accessories at the KWID bungalow (right).**

OPPOSITE **Why hold up a tabletop with four legs when you can raise it with a giant lotus leaf instead? The dining room of my former Sycamore Avenue apartment.**

"The best
details
don't take
themselves
too seriously."

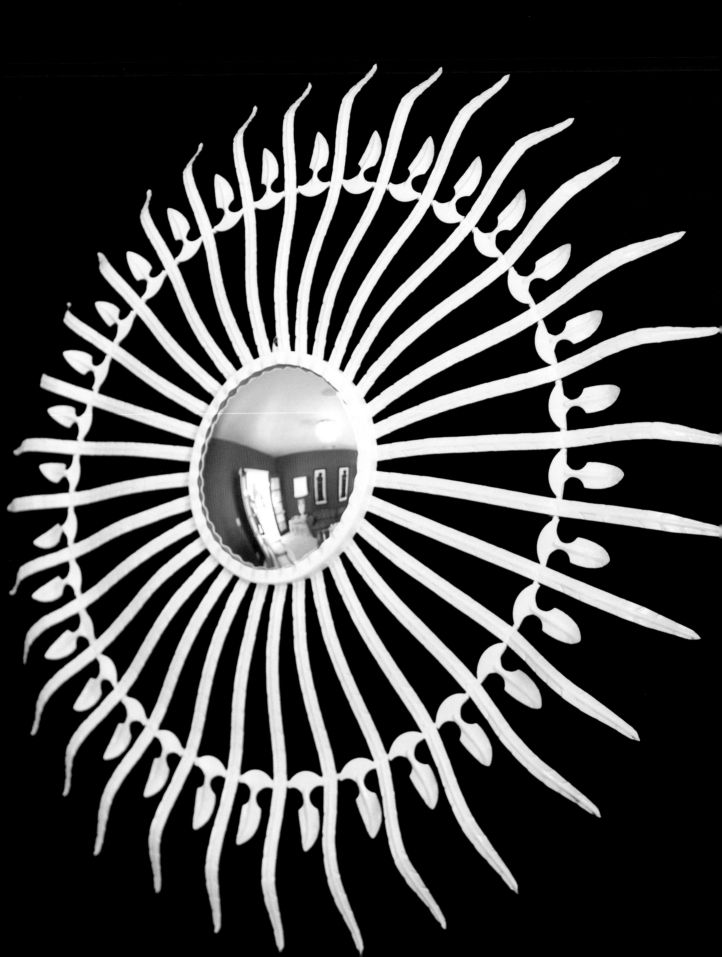

From Moldings to Mosaics

ARCHITECTURAL DETAILS

So many buildings (both new structures and grand old dames) have been disappointingly stripped of great architectural millwork, either for theoretical simplicity, to save money, or for other reasons. But I see them as more than mere seams between floors and walls—they're the built details that lend polish, finish, and quality to a space, inside and out. I've been lucky enough to work on job sites with some of these architectural details and liberally add them if I can. On many projects, I use what I like to call "big ass" base moldings; they're a witty way to make a small room look like it's wearing high heels and has higher ceilings. I'm also fond of substantial casing around doors, as well as wainscoting, beadboard, and wall and ceiling medallions "repurposed" on furniture. Besides adding a visual graphic, classic construction detailing can be a great budget booster. Walls without a lot of artwork can benefit from boiserie paneling, which becomes the art itself. And when the bottom line can't accommodate molding that's custom milled for a taller profile, I'll specify MDF (medium density fiberboard composite, the sausage of wood) plank plus an inexpensive baby molding atop it for a nice finish.

SURFACE MATERIALS

If you only think of hard-surface floors as the ground beneath carpet, think again. They add a layer of detail. Wood installation creates another opportunity for enhancement. I particularly love herringbone tongue-and-groove floors as a complete floor pattern and as an inlay, but there are also many wood species with naturally detailed grain that look beautiful laid in traditional planks. When wood isn't the right choice, tile and marble add an amazing opportunity for detailing. There are truly unlimited selections for every budget and style, far beyond the obvious choices a local flooring store offers. European and antique tile can be ornately painted and glazed; more often, I like a clean, well-made tile set in a detailed pattern, such as chevron, herringbone, or basket weave. For elegant character, I select marble with very beautiful veining, and specify fine lip work like double ogee, bull-nose, and square edges.

Whether it's as simple as a crown molding or a dramatic mosaic masterpiece, embrace the detail in background texture, and most of all, have fun with it.

OVERLEAF **An optical vintage mirror at Estrella gazes upon the Spa quiet room like a wide-open eye with long lashes.**

OPPOSITE **The structure housing the Viceroy may be mid-twentieth century modern, but stately architectural millwork and elegant marble and mirror surfaces add antique essence to the hotel's Cameo Bar.**

Rich grain, deep stain, and glossy polish lend even more interest to the herrringbone-patterneed hardwood floors in the Brentwood estate living room.

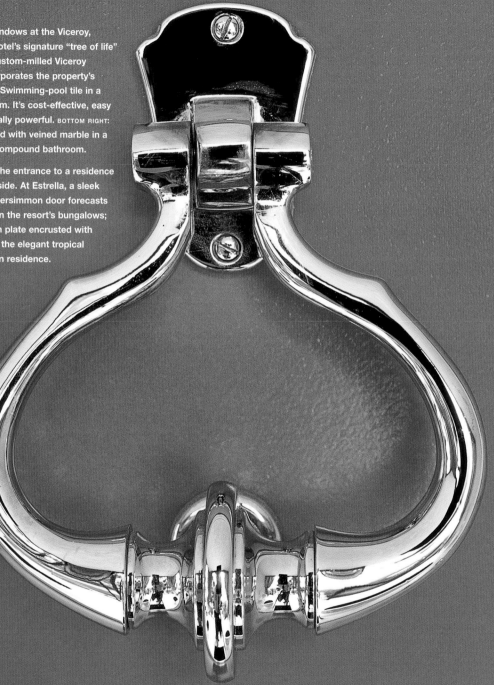

PREVIOUS SPREAD, LEFT

TOP LEFT: A kaleidoscopic Italian wool area rug at the Hollywood Boulevard compound. BOTTOM LEFT: Limed and stained driftwood-esque flooring at the Viceroy is a subtle reminder that the hotel is steps from the Pacific. TOP AND BOTTOM RIGHT: Mosaic floor and wall tile moves the eye at the Avalon Hotel.

PREVIOUS SPREAD, RIGHT

TOP LEFT: Lobby-level windows at the Viceroy, sandblasted with the hotel's signature "tree of life" graphic. BOTTOM LEFT: Custom-milled Viceroy hallway carpeting incorporates the property's caning motif. TOP RIGHT: Swimming-pool tile in a KWID bungalow bathroom. It's cost-effective, easy to maintain, and texturally powerful. BOTTOM RIGHT: Italian mosaic tile paired with veined marble in a Hollywood Boulevard compound bathroom.

THIS PAGE AND OPPOSITE The entrance to a residence can hint at what lies inside. At Estrella, a sleek chrome knocker on a persimmon door forecasts the glow and glamour in the resort's bungalows; a doorknob escutcheon plate encrusted with mosaic shell alludes to the elegant tropical mood of the Rising Glen residence.

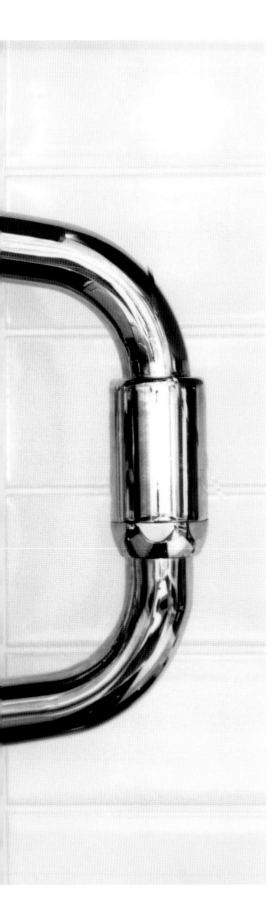

Elements of Style

Just because something in my environment is small or utilitarian doesn't mean it has to be standard or hidden. I like to take ordinary things in every home or office, make them more visually worthy, and add extraordinary touches where commonplace ones are the norm.

HARDWARE

The KWID library is loaded with books and catalogs about one of the world's least glamorous topics: hardware and equipment. From the absolutely minute (like exposed screws) to slightly more visible (vent covers) to even bigger (indestructible stainless-steel prison toilets), I search high and low for cool utilitarian products that bring distinction, spirit, and character to my designs. For example, I've mounted antique casters to chairs so that they look more luxurious or period-specific; their newfound mobility is a definite plus. Another favorite hardware makeover I love: replacing skimpy surface bolts on French doors with hand-forged European ones or extra long brilliant chrome rods. Besides being easier to slide, they look stately and add eye candy to the tops and bottoms of the doors themselves.

In new-build or gut renovations, the KWID team is always on the lookout for opportunities to carry through our design intentions. We've often specified that outlets and switches be installed horizontally rather than vertically to follow the lines of molding or tiling. And when a new heating, ventilating, and air-conditioning system is installed, I choose an interesting cut-metal HVAC grill over a boring off-the-shelf model.

"Copper, brass, iron, nickel, chrome, brushed, or antiqued?"

Soup's on: a pot-filler mounted behind the stovetop at the Brentwood estate.

PLATING AND FINISH

Don't forget that plating and finish are also details. Copper, brass, nickel, iron, chrome, smooth, brushed, antique, or matte? I look carefully at the options, and if I can't find an item in the metal or polish that works, I have it replated or custom-made. In fact, I recently found an amazing brass giraffe, but the job I chose him for is not about gold, so I'm having him dipped in chrome. (He's more of an accessory detail than a functional one, but more about that later!)

Without corner pieces and handles on its many drawers, this expansive vanity at the *House & Garden* showcase home in Los Angeles might have looked like a bank of negative space. The shiny, eye-catching hardware I specified defines its functional elements and breaks up the otherwise flat field.

OPPOSITE, TOP LEFT: **Mod octagonal chromed handles custom-designed by KWID for armoires at the Viceroy.** BOTTOM LEFT: **To offset the deep wood wardrobe doors in the Hollywood Boulevard compound, I used a pair of vintage almond-shaped chrome handles inset with opalescent abalone shell.** TOP RIGHT: **A cabinet at the Rising Glen residence. The face is covered in rough Madagascar cloth; its sleek knobs are smooth polished chrome.** BOTTOM RIGHT AND THIS PAGE: **Details that say KWID: a Viceroy door knocker and massive knob on the front door of my offices.**

"One small item can give rise to a bigger story."

124

UPHOLSTERY, FABRIC, AND FINISHES

I really pay attention to the construction, finish, and trim when using fabric. Pillows, lampshades, and window treatments are just a few items that get the KWID treatment. The right cushion design—envelope, box, or bolster—can make or break the most valuable chair; the wrong finish on a fabric (like a corded edge where a self-welt would do) can also detract from a piece.

Whatever the budget, durability should always be a concern. I always specify a hardwood frame and eight-way hand-tied springs so the piece will stand the test of time and tush. Cushions and pillows can be stuffed with down, made from synthetics, or filled with a combination of both. For hotel and commercial projects, we evenly mix down and feathers, since down on its own separates too quickly. Residential clients usually prefer down's cushy quality, but many people are allergic to it and ask for synthetic fill. Mattresses also vary in construction and firmness. I ask residential clients about their preference but specify a firmer mattress for hospitality projects. And both in hotels and at home, we always add protective sheaths underneath pillowcases, fitted sheets, and duvet covers to ward off allergens and dust mites.

The purists and grumblers of the world may not think things such as these are beneficial. But if you've ever sat on a couch with sagging springs, noticed spreading seams on a boring cushion, or glimpsed drool-stained ticking on a bed pillow, you'll probably agree with me—they're a must!

PREVIOUS AND FOLLOWING SPREADS **Eye of the needle: Interesting embroidery, passementerie, tassels, beads, and seams can add bold statements to basic surfaces.**

OPPOSITE **Well-made vintage furniture and fabrics are often better investments than brand-new purchases from a showroom floor, as these 1960s calfskin loungers in the Hollywood Boulevard compound attest. Discovered in London, where they once enhanced the Czech embassy, their quality craftsmanship and classic design still endure.**

Equipped for Glamour

Unlike other rooms, bathrooms, kitchens, and closets have pretty explicit uses. But as with hardware, upholstery, and other utilitarian tools, they deserve dignity in their details. The experience one has in these rooms—a long shower after a hard day, Sunday morning brunch preparation, dressing for an important night out—can be life's most pleasurable. It's both the visual and hidden elements that can make it so.

KITCHENS

I aim for kitchens that are beautiful as well as useful. The overall functionality of the kitchen depends on a client's needs. For serious cooks, we might choose commercial ranges and refrigerators, stovetop pot-filler faucets that pipe water to large tureens right atop the range, custom-designed pull-out drawers with special racks and dowels, and other industrial tools. In less busy kitchens, we often remove upper cabinets altogether to open up the room, and add windows or artwork. The only rule of thumb is cleanliness. Use liquid soap in dispensers, and if possible, install them beneath the countertop to keep the surface clutter-free.

BATHS

Who wants to walk into a bathroom and see a grimy toothbrush, a greasy comb, and half-full shampoo bottles on display? Bathrooms and the details within them should impart a feeling of cleanliness and freshness. I design many niches in shower and bath walls to conceal bottles within the architecture, yet still keep supplies close at hand. I'm also a big fan of long and exaggerated handles on shower doors to make a design statement and get a good grip when hands are wet. As for countertops, it's best to leave them unfettered by drugstore paraphernalia—use drawers and medicine cabinets for those items, and mount makeup mirrors directly on vanities or walls. Mix up bathroom accessories (soap dish, tissue cover, perfume tray, toothbrush holder, and so on); matched sets are frightening and unnecessary, as are lint-catching colored towels and floor mats, and pastel tissues and toilet paper.

OPPOSITE **The Brentwood estate's sunlit kitchen combines industrial tools, such as a recessed paper towel roll and a Viking bread and plate warmer, with palatial marble floors and countertops.**

OVERLEAF **In bathrooms, forgo monotonously matching soap dishes and toothbrush holders. Instead, store towels in open cabinets, recesses, and cubby holes, and tuck grooming items away in collectible vases and vintage apothecary jars.**

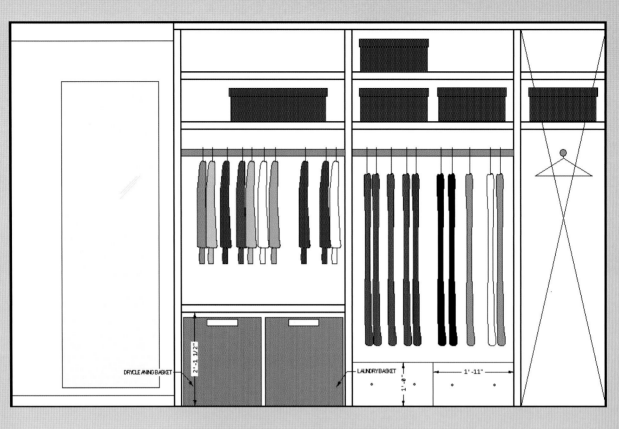

DRYCLE ANING BASKET

2'-1 1/2"

LAUNDRY BASKET

1'-0"

1'-11"

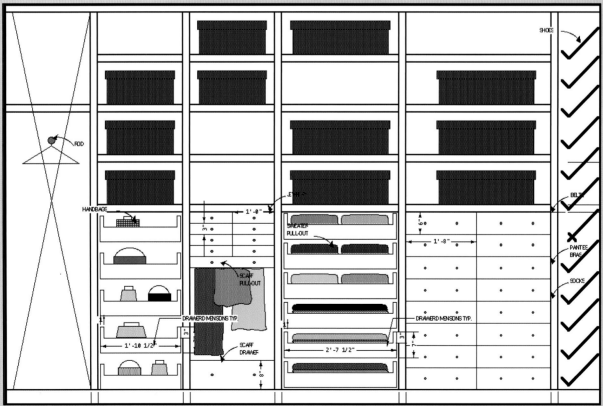

ROD

HANDBAGS

JEWEL Y

1'-0"

3"

SWEATER
PULL-OUT

SCARF
PULL-OUT

DRAWERD MENSDINS TYP.

1'-10 1/2"

3"

SCARF
DRAWER

8"

2'-7 1/2"

3"

DRAWERD MENSDINS TYP.

9"

1'-8"

3"

7"

SHOES

BELTS

PANTIES
BRAS

SOCKS

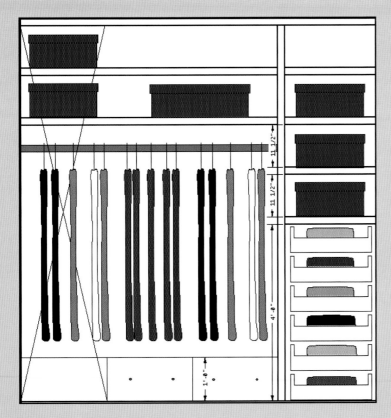

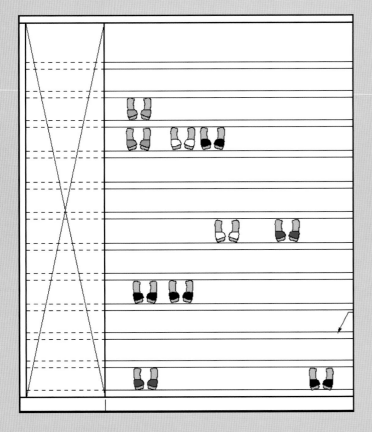

CLOSETS AND STORAGE

Inside closets and cabinets, the most crucial details include good lighting and versatility. An efficient and welcoming storage area can feel like a personal boutique each time you dress, display, or organize. Windowless walk-in wardrobes really eat up lighting, especially ones paneled in dark woods or cedar. I design closets with appropriate light sources or increase the bulb wattage when I cannot remodel. To organize clothing, linens, and other personal belongings, I go wild with hooks and racks, baskets for dry cleaning, laundry and hand-wash, plus shelved dividers to keep shoes, handbags, and luggage from scratching one another. In smaller spaces, simple stacking boxes are also efficient, especially when depth or height are lacking. Do you want an unexpected flash of color and texture that won't interfere with your wardrobe? Try wallpaper on the ceiling of your closet to jazz it up.

A view of the four walls of the woman's wardrobe in the Brentwood estate master bedroom. This walnut mega-closet includes tricked-out drawers for draped scarves, sunglasses, and handbags; baskets for laundry and dry cleaning; a shoe wall; and a refrigerator. It's lit by crystal chandeliers and features a floating center island with a built-in ottoman.

The Art of Detail

134

As a designer, I deal with peoples' personal collections every day. Some clients come to me with priceless art and antiques. Others have sports memorabilia, platinum records, and family photos. Really, the best details are unexpected ones that don't take themselves too seriously.

I try to supplement, pare down, and organize the accessories that my clients and I have selected. For purely aesthetic details, I look for objects and works that are more figural or have a great graphic effect or textural appeal. Sculptural elements, such as a backlit object where a small lamp might be expected, can be particularly inviting. My very favorite accessories not only add dimensional layers and colors, they tell tales you can't find in any storybook.

"I embellish upon and carry through what I already have."

Whatever you enjoy collecting, don't display a swarm of same-sized pieces together. Alternate scale and texture, especially when grouping monochromatic items like the bowl and ceramic eggs in my former Sycamore Avenue apartment living room. I also hung a disassembled four-panel floor screen on the wall to further vary the scale and to unify the otherwise empty expanse.

LEFT **If a space is too vast for anything other than an extensive art collection, use ornate design details instead. This suite at the Viceroy uses reflective wallpaper, mirrors, molding, a mobile-like chandelier, and a single well-placed oil painting in lieu of a gallery's worth of canvases.**

RIGHT **Simply sophisticated: White footstools with yellow cushions are balanced by a profusion of matching tulips and other accessories in the Rising Glen residence foyer.**

"Details add the layers and layers add the interest."

ARTWORK

Very few projects involve trips to Sotheby's or the Wildenstein Galleries to pick up showpieces to hang here and there. Rather than impractically advocating the works of the world's masters, I take a much more realistic approach to the display of art. As I've already discussed, wallcoverings, paneling, and applied moldings add instant layers to long expanses of walls and are textural when juxtaposed with paintings and prints. For placement, I like to extend a monochromatic palette when hanging art over wallpaper; it finishes a room so nicely. Also, I generally base art installation on what surrounds it. Matching colors and textures, or pitting them against each other, can really energize a section of a room or a whole space.

The frame or pedestal I select is as important as the piece it holds or elevates. Other than not overpowering what's being set off, I'm never limited by conventions about framing and mounting. Use any border size—don't be shy about isolating a tiny picture with a huge mat. Try trading mounting board for a mirror, or look into a floated frame that makes the art magically hover inside its borders. It's always a plus to see a room that successfully mixes artwork, objects, and diverse display methods.

PREVIOUS SPREAD, LEFT **Personality-laden design details in the Cameo Bar at Viceroy–from wingback chairs to embroidered griffins to Lucite tabletops–are as layered and nuanced as a character in a novel.**

OPPOSITE **Solar flair: A split abstract oil from the 1970s harmonizes with the flame-stitch upholstery and brass finishes in the Lasky Drive medical suite sitting room.**

142

FLOWERS AND PLANTS

If you collect dried and fake flowers, you're going to collect dust. I do not care for potpourri, massive silk floral arrangements, freeze-dried wreaths and swags, and the like. Better to have one single stem that's a fragrant gift of the earth than five dozen red roses that will never die. Similarly, potted plants are best used in small doses, with the exception of well-tended terraces, sunrooms, and greenhouses. Good design doesn't need houseplants; if they aren't a symptom of bad design, they're definitely a Band-Aid for it.

There are a few plants and flowers that I use regularly and prize for their elegance and grace: regal phalaenopsis orchids, lush pussy willows, forgiving and easy-to-grow azaleas, majestic bamboo, and spring-blooming cherry blossoms. For even more detail, I like to use a painted bamboo stake in the floral arrangement and cover soil with moss, bark, pebbles, or even marbles.

If they're not real, why have them? Fresh flowers at the Hollywood Boulevard compound.

What Lights My Fire

STIMULI

148

One of my most-used expressions is "last Tuesday."

It pretty much says it all about what sparks my imagination and ideas: if it's everywhere and it's tired, it's not for me. I'm always seeking out the original, the overlooked, and the off-center to inspire me personally and professionally.

I don't like to take myself too seriously, but I do think about what inspires me and finds a way into my work. I'm a very sensitive person with an imagination that works overtime. It's gotten me far in my career, but can keep me up at night, too. So when I get a complimentary comment or letter from one of my peers in the creative world, it always gives me a huge boost. I keep a collection of notes sent by everyone, from vendors and students to editors and colleagues. It reminds me that I'm fortunate to have so many people pulling for me and helping me to realize my vision.

Mankind has been around for so long, and aesthetically, everything has already been done. I have a library full of magazines and out-of-print art books, and I always find something in them to captivate me. I can't get enough information about the timeless and sophisticated work of design genius David Hicks, who coined the term "tablescape." I'm fascinated by the decadent Asian sensibility of costume, set, and jewelry designer Tony Duquette, and the sublime modernism of furniture and interiors genius Arthur Elrod. I admire the American decorating masters Parish-Hadley (for their simultaneously patrician and modern feel) and Billy Baldwin (a fellow Southerner with a reverence for color). I'm always moved by the color and texture of Mark Rothko's paintings. Absorbing cultural and decorative history helps me look to the past to create something unexpected and new for the future.

As fanatical as I am about design, I have to escape from the studio as much as possible to ignite my brain. There's so much out there to discover. Whether I'm traveling abroad, visiting museums and galleries at home, bargaining for an amazing find, or lavishing attention on my loved ones, I never stop exploring the arts, cultures, and people that keep my creative fuse blazing.

PREVIOUS SPREAD **For most KWID designs, I can cite personal inspirations, memories, and experiences that influence the finished product or composition. The seductive chair (left) designed for the Viceroy guest rooms and dynamic sofa fabrics (right) selected for Estrella always remind me of past haunts and jaunts. Without that emotional resonance, my work would feel empty and impersonal.**

OPPOSITE **Take us home! A pair of fabulous lounge chairs catches my eye on the street in New York.**

ANTIQUES

OVER 100
ANTIQUE DEALERS

The
New York
Antique Center

30 FEET ACROSS STR

"I carry a sketchbook wherever I go in case inspiration strikes."

152

PREVIOUS SPREAD, LEFT,
THIS PAGE, AND OPPOSITE
**Journal sketches from
jaunts through London
and Paris and vacations
in former European
colonies in southeast
Asia and the Caribbean.
These trips helped
crystallize my visions
for Viceroy and Estrella.**

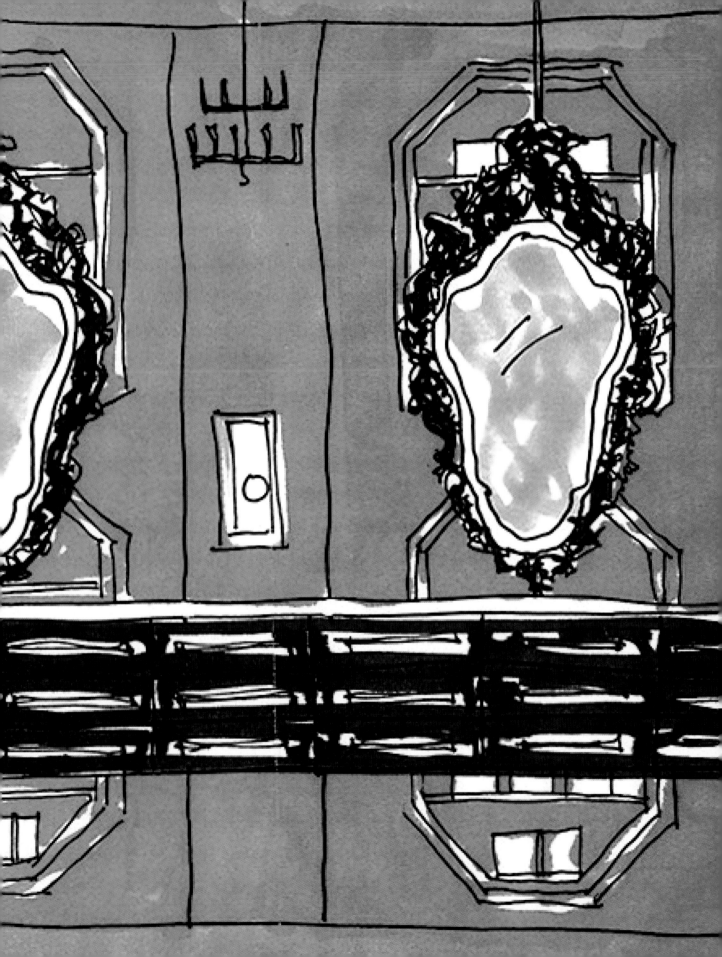

Window Shopping the World: Cambodia to Capri

Of all the experiences in my life—childhood, art school, and professional practice—nothing has influenced my creative perspective as much as traveling. Expeditions in foreign countries and famous American cities (where everything looks, sounds, smells, and tastes unique) are always thrilling, whether you're in a five-star hotel or at a street bazaar. I'm fortunate to have journeyed through Europe and the Mediterranean; into parts of North Africa, Southeast Asia, and the Far East; and across North America and the Caribbean. Next on my list are South America, India, and Africa. It's a great package; not only do I travel specifically on business, I can incorporate my globe-trotting experiences into my designs afterward.

Finding shops when I'm traveling is as much art as science. First of all, I don't buy anything in hotel shops (unless I need an instant-gratification fix), and I avoid tourist shops that hawk trinkets and T-shirts. I collect articles about particular cities from magazines over time, and then bring them along on my trips. I read tons of travel guides and rip pages out of them so I don't have to lug the whole book. Then, upon arrival at my destination, I look in the phone directory in my hotel room. Finally, some of the best tips come by word of mouth. If you are traveling in a third-world country, ask the concierge at your hotel for assistance in hiring a guide who is shopping-savvy, and ask the shopkeepers you meet for referrals to other vendors. Most important, trust your instincts. If something looks intriguing from outside of a shop window—even if it doesn't resemble a regular storefront—check it out if the location is safe and you're not alone. If you are traveling solo, you may not want to take chances in a risky area.

OPPOSITE AND FOLLOWING SPREAD **Accessories one is able to tote home can be worth the trip. I once carried a twenty-four-inch ceramic elephant across Southeast Asia because I didn't want to risk shipping it back. I'm totally comfortable shipping a container full of goods back from Europe but a bit wary of more exotic ports of call. FedEx and UPS are great for smaller items, and you'll have instant gratification when you get home!**

"Finding shops when traveling is as much art as science."

My shopping excursions for Estrella took me from Palm Springs (where I rescued the ceramic whippets that became models for the dogs guarding each room) to Palm Beach (the source for some outrageous woven fiberglass patio furniture). Other unusual finds included the Popsicle-like armchair, hoofed table, and ceramic amphora.

Your Slip Is Showing

Fashion is definitely an influence on my designs, but current trends or things that quickly appear dated are not. I look more to texture, color, or graphic fabric or construction. Like any gal, I buy clothing and accessories for my body as well as for their relevance to my work. As a designer, I do want to look stylish.

Traveling is a prime source for amazing fashion finds. How people dress in foreign countries is fascinating, because so many garments have religious, class, or other symbolic meanings. Even though people probably thought I was an idiot, I wore a woven grass hat in Vietnam to shade my face; only field-workers wear them there. I wanted a monk's jacket from Burma but couldn't chase one down. Only by seeing these unique articles firsthand can you really understand the inspirations for great fashion designers over time.

Back in the Westernized world, I'm inspired as much by vintage clothing and jewelry as by current styles. I'll see a tie or a vintage dress in an intriguing fabric and buy it for a textile or carpet inspiration; or I might see a period color combination on a classic jacket that sets off an idea. Oversized jewelry (both valuable and costume) gives me great images for chandeliers and hardware. Like interior design, fashion design is a disciplined blend of art and commerce, and I admire the work of Sigerson Morrison and Marc Jacobs, and the resurrection of classic fashion houses like Gucci and Yves Saint Laurent.

"My design work influences my wardrobe and vice-versa."

My design work influences my wardrobe choices and vice versa. Clothing construction can spark a concept for tailoring upholstery; a metallic hardware finish might inspire me to wear gold- or silver-toned accessories.

"Animal accessories call out to me every time I go shopping."

Aesthetic Quackery

I can go anywhere to see one of the most inspiring things on the planet—animals. Besides being innocent and honest, their bodies are so sculptural and their fur, skin, feathers, and scales are beautifully textural and colorful. The hues that I see on fish and sea turtles when scuba diving are incredible and certainly motivate me to work with strong color palettes.

I also use a lot of animal forms as accessories to temper a room that may seem too forbidding or too decorative. Animals really lighten things up a little and enrich our spaces. It seems as though some animal piece calls out to me every time I go shopping. I guess they know that I'll give them a good home.

Animals are more than props in my life. I am a supporter of and fund-raiser for Best Friends Animal Sanctuary, a Utah haven for abused and neglected dogs, cats, horses, and wildlife in need of a new home or shelter. I also support the Humane Society and Muttmatchers in their work to help four-footed folks who can't always help themselves.

At the end of the day, a beautifully designed room is a lot more special if someone is there wagging his tail when you come through the door.

OVERLEAF **In my office at the KWID bungalow, I softened this robust horse sculpture's mighty stance with a flock of tiny brass birds.**

OPPOSITE **I get on a roll with an animal toward which I gravitate, and suddenly I'll find that species represented in every decorative accessory! Of course, none of them compares to my mutt, Brea, whom I found on the street in Los Angeles and brought home for a better life.**

ECLECTICISM

The term *eclecticism* is thrown around a lot in design publications and discussion these days. The traditional definition of an eclectic room would be one that combines a lot of different eras, styles, and elements selected from various sources.

However, KWID doesn't really do things according to traditional definitions. Unless I was being painfully polite, I would never label an interior "eclectic" just because it was made up of miscellaneous furniture and fabrics. To me, eclecticism produces excitement through creative tension. Eclectic interiors may startle you at first, but it's that surprising quality that holds you there and calls you back again. An eclectic room challenges you to look a little closer at what's going on, and to try to solve a visual riddle there. Eclectic elements don't strive to be unexpected—they just are.

I create that tension in my designs with aesthetic juxtapositions and contradictions. This decorative chemistry can be as subtle as media differences between accessories (like pairing crude metalwork with glossy ceramics), or more notable visual friction, like pairing an Empire table and a mid-twentieth-century chair. If the project calls for it, I also combine crown, base, and door moldings of various heights and profiles in the same room to eliminate monotony.

While I always push myself to find new ways to invent environments that stimulate and challenge expectations, I don't consciously go for an over-the-top effect. Even a room with very vivid contrasts should be a timeless and pleasurable place to work, play, relax, and live. Don't just look for eclectic statements with your eyes. Look with your mind and your imagination.

PREVIOUS SPREAD **Combine intense colors in the same family. The rich reds, oranges and pinks in the Hollywood Boulevard compound master bedroom and a Maison 140 guest suite are perfectly compatible because they are variants of the same stunning shade.**

OPPOSITE **Blend soft and severe. In the Hollywood Boulevard compound living room, flat industrial concrete surrounding the fireplace harmonizes with the room's deeply polished wooden floors and window frames, while sweeping fringed greens on the hearth play against a compact trio of decorative artichokes on the coffee table.**

"Eclecticism produces excitement through creative tension."

Calculated Risks

Despite someone's best intentions to stir things up in a space, a wild array of materials may not look very fresh. I find that choosing a few ideas, then comparing and contrasting them, is much more effective than throwing a hundred different decorative ingredients into one room.

It can be strangely insightful to look back at past projects and see patterns emerge in my design. In fact, many of the KWID basics and trademarks I've explored in earlier chapters become important elements for making an eclectic interior composition. So before you start festooning your interior with classic midcentury Charles Eames chairs, antique French chandeliers, and South American pottery, stop for a moment and consider some of the more fundamental factors that you can use to create an exciting and eclectic interior.

PREVIOUS SPREAD **Transcend time and cross the continents. A proper neoclassical fireplace surround, probably original to the apartment's construction in the 1930s, effortlessly shares space with an African Zebra skin rug, antique Asian armchair, and modern mirrored hearth screen.**

OPPOSITE **Plan your work and work your plan. I could fearlessly combine forms and textures of varying aesthetic lineage in this KWID bungalow bathroom by using a monochromatic color base as my starting point.**

Take a textile to the limit. Several types of cowhide, including a split grain woven leather rug, Napa leather lounge chairs, a suede ottoman, and nubuck chair cushions, make a complete statement in this conversation corner of the Hollywood Boulevard compound.

Think every choice through.
In the Brentwood estate
living room, an intentional
mix of periods and
styles–from rococo to French
Empire to art deco and
beyond–takes stylistic
tension right to the edge; a
specific gold-and-white color
way holds everything steady.

Agree to Disagree

There doesn't have to be an agreeable relationship between a building's exterior architecture, its interior design, and the activities that occur in and around it. In fact, there's something oppressive about an environment that is too uniform.

Since most of my projects are gut renovations of existing structures, changing the overall architectural style is almost never an option. Instead, I take advantage of the property's original bone structure, and either echo it throughout the design direction or counter it entirely. This disparity between the outside and inside is the guest's first clue that unexpected spectacles will unfold throughout his or her experience in a KWID interior.

Aesthetic nonconformity between exterior and interior is especially appealing in professional spaces. I really love transforming an office space that on the outside feels totally anonymous yet is so distinctive within. In today's business world, where so many people are challenged to "think outside of the box," it's especially important to go to work in a space that provokes new ways of thinking and problem solving. That warm little box might feel safe, but it's my job to help pry you out of it before you suffocate!

The Century Park West investment offices are inside a modern building in one of Los Angeles' busiest commercial areas. Step out of the elevator, though, and you're in a most regal setting. I created a deluxe, old-world feel with liberal use of gold leaf, rich walnut panels finished with French polish, and elegant natural materials including velvet, lamb's wool, and suede.

Masculine-Feminine

Some interiors have that almost indescribable emotional friction people call "chemistry." In my designs, I often explore the bounds of the sexes by blending elements that are usually associated only with one gender or the other, or only with someone of a certain age. While this relationship frequently crops up in projects created for a husband and wife, it's also a factor in designing workplaces, hotels, and spaces for individuals of either sex.

I believe that everyone shares both male and female traits and characteristics, and that themes and interests considered particularly "feminine" or "masculine" appeal to all of us. And at the same time, I think children have an inherent adult wisdom, just as adults can express refreshingly childlike opinions and desires. For so many centuries, our culture has punished or ostracized people who don't fit the stereotypical role of man, woman, or child. Design can liberate us from those limitations, and I hope that my interiors continue to question and redraw these boundaries.

"A room with vivid contrasts can be timeless and pleasing."

To appeal to both men and women, many spas bathe everything in an innocuous beige or sage color scheme. But for the spa at Estrella, we stuck with the hotel's white, yellow, and black motif, and even shaded this post-treatment quiet room in his-and-hers black-and-white.

PREVIOUS SPREAD, LEFT **A lady's lair: My former Sycamore Avenue apartment was a study in strength and seductiveness. A comely East Asian statue presides over brooding ebonized woods and sexy golden silks.**

PREVIOUS SPREAD, RIGHT **In the living room of one of the Canon Villas–luxury residential townhouses for itinerant executives temporarily based in Beverly Hills–deliberate fundamentals like scale, color, and texture lie behind more abstract themes, like the interplay of the sexes.**

LEFT **Liz, meet Dick: In the lobby at Estrella, serious chemistry between a fainting couch covered in striped silk and a Regency-style chair upholstered in black leather.**

190

PREVIOUS SPREAD, LEFT
British bus-destination roll art and wood objets in the KWID bungalow kitchen.

PREVIOUS SPREAD, RIGHT
A multicultural accessory mix in the Green Bay Road penthouse guest bedroom.

RIGHT **My former bedroom on Sycamore Avenue is part men's haberdashery shop, part women's couture salon. The walls are aubergine, while pops of magenta put some lipstick in the palette.**

Fantasy in Decoration

STAGECRAFT

When you enter a building or pass from room to room, the experience can be as dazzling as the black-and-white to Technicolor transition Dorothy experienced between Kansas and the Land of Oz.

When I enter a space, I want to be moved—I want to feel the drama.

The famous MGM musical *The Wizard of Oz* made a major impression on me as a child. Dorothy's dog, Toto; the Cowardly Lion; and those coveted ruby slippers are particularly vivid recollections. Growing up in the 1970s, I was mesmerized by *The Sonny and Cher Comedy Hour*'s ever-changing sets and Bob Mackie outfits. In each episode, everything revolved around color and change, from the songs and the costumes to the spotlights to the wild sets.

Today, creating emotional and visual excitement like a great film does is a KWID must. My work in production definitely helped pushed my perceptions and shaped my interiors. In set design, the scenes tell the audience a story: about its characters, their time and place, and even about the viewers themselves. Every set is slightly different, because every scene evokes moods of varying degrees.

A big design project is a lot like a movie or play production. Many of the same players get the job done, from the electrician wiring the lights and the carpenter building the backdrop, to the costumer styling the actors' wardrobe and the property master in charge of their props. The role of the director falls to me. And just like on a set, the cast and crew do make outrageous demands, yell and argue, and order cappuccinos!

Most clients are nervous about adding high drama to their homes, because they think it will make too much of a statement. But we can design the space so it looks, and feels, wonderful at completion. One spouse might say, "We want a dark, old smoking-room vibe," while the other says, "How about French Regency?" Then, it's my eye and instinct that infuses the mix with glamour, sophistication, and harmony. Interior drama isn't about overstyling. It's about taking risks.

PREVIOUS SPREAD, LEFT **A guest room door at Viceroy: A bright color on a front entrance really draws you in, like an intriguing movie poster or film titles.**

PREVIOUS SPREAD, RIGHT **"I'm ready for my close-up, Mr. DeMille": This animated ceramic greyhound stands sentry at the KWID bungalow.**

OPPOSITE **At the Brentwood estate, an arching staircase is center stage in the entry hall; I like to imagine a beautifully attired woman sweeping down those steps to greet her guests in a moment out of *The Philadelphia Story*.**

Different Sets for Different Acts

In schematic design, whether I'm blocking out a floor plan, selecting color swatches, installing furniture, or placing objects, I look at my settings through an imaginary viewfinder or frame as though I'm planning a scene for a shoot. This doesn't just mean putting things in place to freeze a sterile portrait in time—it's a way to create stages where experiences can be played out. There are different rooms for different functions, and those activities form the story lines in our daily lives.

The tools for building and shaping these sets vary from job to job and room to room. With a gut renovation, my options include architectural modifications, like removing walls and redesigning staircases. Even without the luxury of remodeling, I can build a quasi stage using large elements like screens that block out movement and focus the eye on a specific area.

Traveling from room to room doesn't bring the curtain down but rather marks a change of scene. The materials for making that transition—color, texture, furnishings, and so on—can be pronounced or subtle. Keep in mind that sound, temperature, and aromas can also migrate from place to place and really kill a carefully composed moment. Insulation (whether it's professionally installed polyurethane foam in the walls or a pair of heavy curtains) is a key tool for ensuring privacy levels on your own personal set.

OPPOSITE **The mirrored screens in the dining room at my former Sycamore Avenue apartment enhanced its intimate Asian jewel box vibe.**

OVERLEAF **At a hotel, all of the common areas are stages for action, whether it's business, romance, celebration, or adventure. Rumor has it that Bar Noir at Maison 140 has become a hot spot for trysting celebrities.**

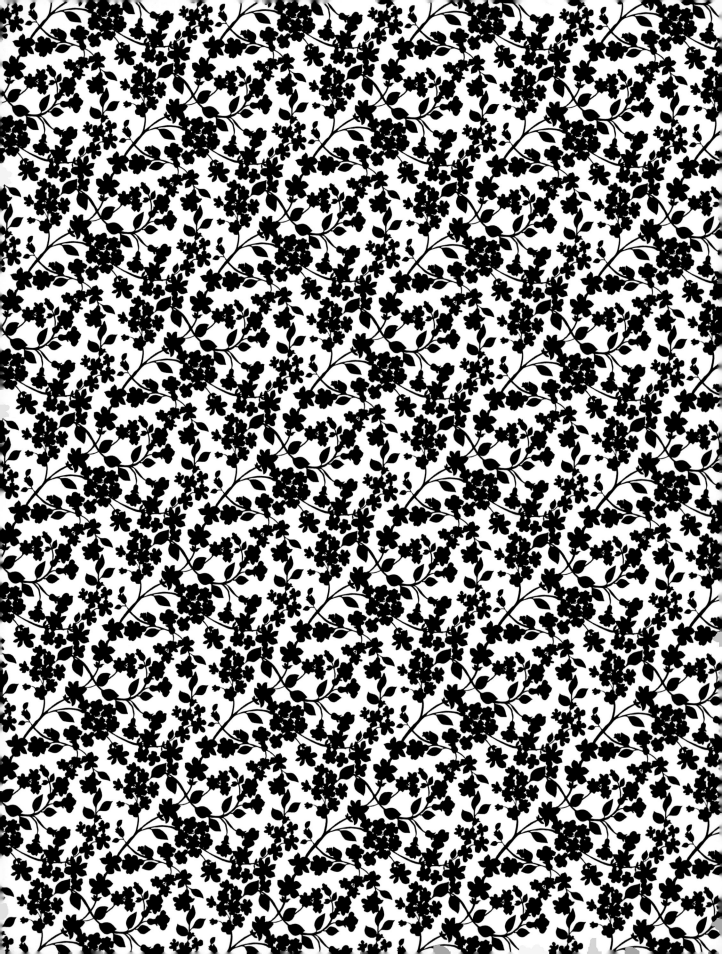

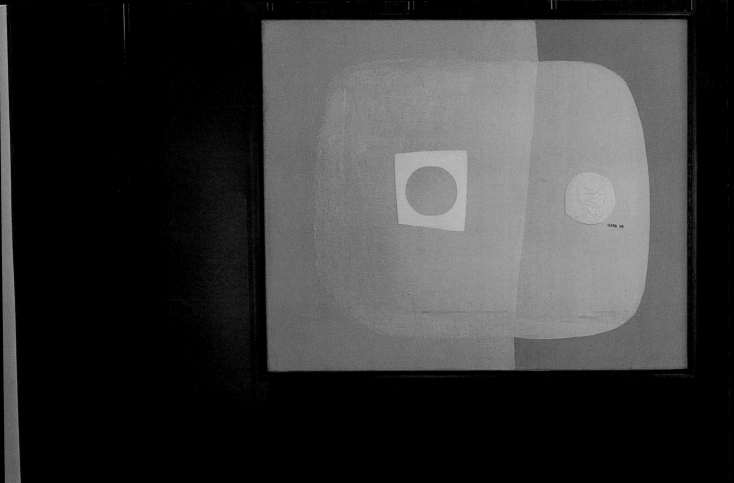

PREVIOUS SPREAD Shadowplay: the long view and an extreme close-up of the silhouetted wallpaper designed for dramatic effect at Estrella.

ABOVE Even without a script, treasures can collaborate for a moment of tabletop theater. At the Hollywood Boulevard compound, a ceramic bird and plated shells beneath a brilliant sun painted in oil secretly salute my childhood.

Allusions to Place, Illusions of Time

206

Few projects allow me to create a theatrical sense of time and place like the design of a hotel interior. For Avalon, the existing mid-twentieth-century architecture set the project's tone. After the space was gutted, we carried the property's historic sensibility through the three adjacent guest room buildings, restaurant, and bar with a mix of my own period-inspired designs, vintage furnishings, select current pieces, and touches that accent California's relaxed patio lifestyle—but the hotel isn't a time capsule. Instead, it's more of a contemporary interpretation of its Hollywood roots, and ultimately something new, fresh, and sexy. I think *Interior Design* nailed it, calling the décor "refreshingly devoid of cliché or kitsch."

The same approach applies at Maison 140. It feels like a chic Parisian hideaway, but it inhabits a traditional Georgian revival town house near the busiest street in Beverly Hills, not a centuries-old landmark on the Left Bank. I used chinoiserie and neobaroque and 1970s modernist touches everywhere, but guests never feel that they're trapped on the set of either *Turandot* (set in China), *Butterfly* (set in Japan), or *Boogie Nights*.

Playing with typical expectations about location and history also helped KWID create the drama of Viceroy. For its backdrop, I merged European colonial decorative elements with contemporary architectural lines; at the same time, the client wanted to reinforce the hotel's beach location. Initially, no one understood what KWID dubbed "modern colonialism." Once we mixed caning patterns and polished chrome, snooty spaniel-shaped lamps and hip Lucite tables, driftwood finishes and Empire-green hues, the story became clear.

Scene study: considering a period accessory at a favorite Los Angeles antique shop.

While not quite as stage directed as my hotel projects, the Brentwood estate is no less dramatic. This gentlemen's den incorporates mid-twentieth-century art and accessories, French polished paneling, and voluptuous couches for its leading man.

OPPOSITE In the Green Bay Road penthouse, pale accessories and a Chippendale chair come alive against the rich walnut bookshelf.

Even with limited funds, there is still a way to bring fantasy to life on a grand scale. At Estrella, I traded the hotel's tired Southwestern vibe for a modern Regency effect using very simple materials. Many of the guest rooms at Estrella are Spanish bungalows; in both Palm Springs and South Florida, there are Mediterranean-style buildings with French Regency–inspired facades that make them look like sets on a studio lot. So instead of scrapping the area's roots, we celebrated its "Hollywood playground" heritage—klieg-light-white paint, stagy drapery and awnings, and an accent pattern with a neoclassic Greek key design.

Since many of my projects allow me to research regions and their decorative histories on location, I get to use shops around the world (and around the corner) as my personal prop houses. But even when budgets are squeezed, I never shop straight out of catalogs. Pore over books, haunt local flea markets, stretch your imagination, but never settle for something you wouldn't give a rave review.

The bar at Estrella serves up old-school resort glamour with a refreshing Hollywood twist. Can't you just smell the lemons, limes, and maraschino cherries?

Pen-and-ink musing on Estrella
staff uniforms. Naughty chambermaid,
Hellenic handmaiden, 1950s homemaker:
hotel uniforms as costumes. Embellishing
central design motifs on standard-issue
garments adds to the hotel story line.

OPPOSITE **An Estrella staff member
in action.**

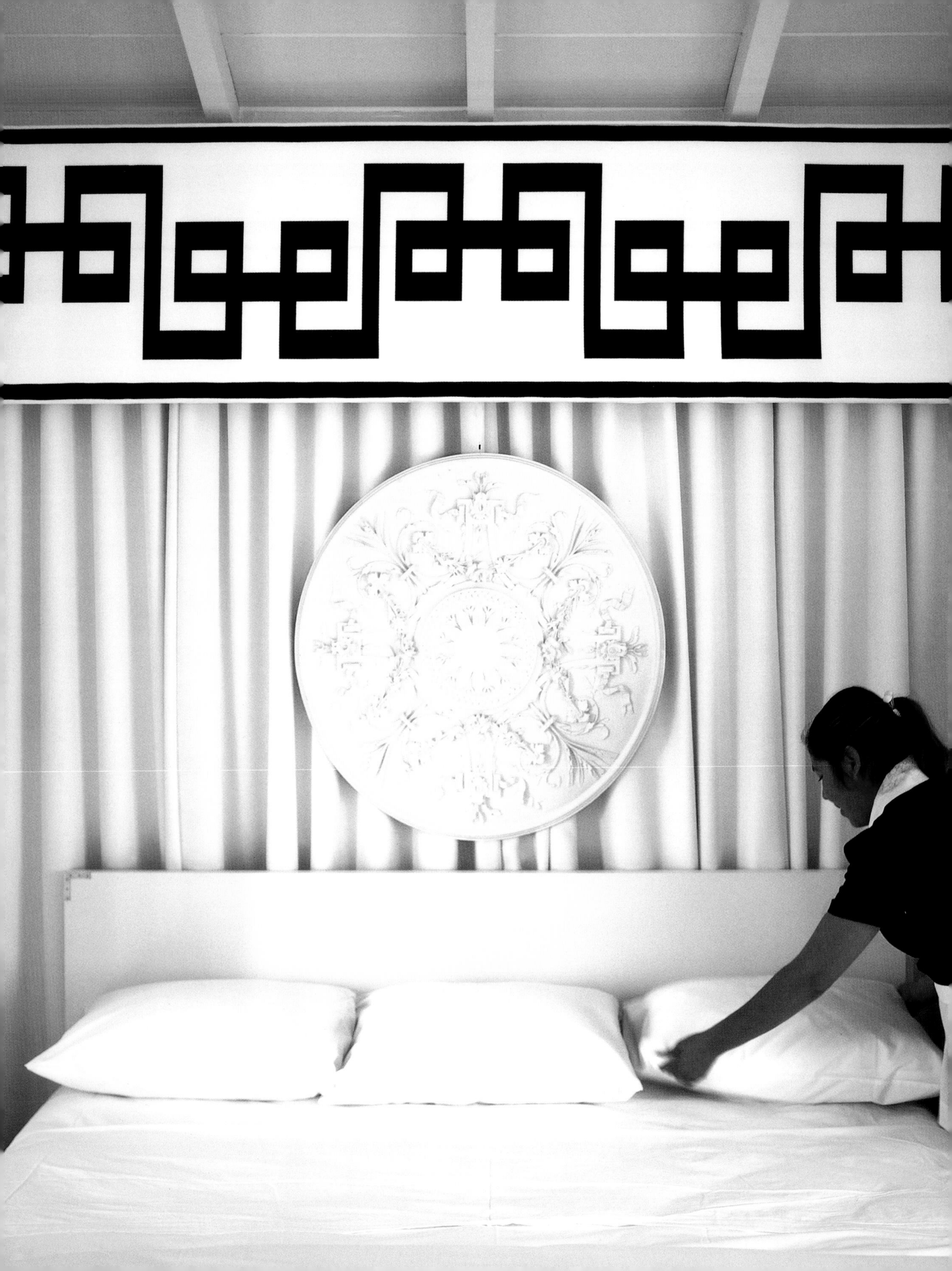

"Inside a room,
I want to
be moved—
I want to feel
the drama."

Visual Trickery

Sometimes one simple element can do more to create an illusion than a thousand antique period pieces. In my designs, that means using light, shadow, and depth of field, often in the most old-school ways. On all of KWID's residential projects, and even many commercial jobs, I use a multitude of wall, ceiling, floor, and table lamps, usually wired with dimmers. They not only help convey a stylistic point of view—like the glamorous KWID-designed crystal chandelier we often use in bathrooms—they also cast a soft cinematic glow that makes people look rested and healthy by eliminating "raccoon eyes" and deemphasizing less-than-toned legs. Darkness can be even more dramatic than light itself: it can evoke a film noir feeling of eternal midnight when natural moonlight is only available part of the day.

When I need to manipulate the depth of an area (whether it's puffing up a small area or putting an exclamation point on a huge one) my first choice is a mirror. Mirrors are available in practically any size and color, and can be antiqued, marbled, and otherwise tweaked for effect. (They also do a great job of covering scarred surfaces and bouncing light around.) Spatial hocus-pocus can go beyond the looking glass: optical patterns on walls and ceilings, oversize moldings, and windows on spacious scenes can also modify your sense of space.

A note of caution about elaborate gestures, whether they involve mirrors, lights, or any other illusory material: I always recommend testing a scale model or other sample before committing to something you might regret later.

PREVIOUS SPREAD, LEFT **Beyond baroque: A reflective tabletop and ornate vanity mirror kaleidoscopically echo the wallpapered ceiling, abstract wall art, and sculpted armchairs in a Maison 140 guest room.**

OPPOSITE **The focal point of the Brentwood estate dressing room vestibule, this mirrored chest of drawers draws the eye, rebounds overhead lighting, and reflects its rich surroundings.**

220

PREVIOUS SPREAD, LEFT **With its lofty 14-foot ceilings and second-story mezzanine level balcony, the dining room in the Rising Glen residence deserved a focal point. So we installed identical orange lanterns to light the room and unite the space below and catwalk above.**

PREVIOUS SPREAD, RIGHT **Candelabrum flickering with warm light provide low-tech mood lighting. Candlesticks and tea lights are much more elegant than huge wax slabs with a dozen wicks.**

RIGHT **Lemon sorbet: In the restaurant at Estrella, mirrors patterned with Regency-inspired graphics reflect the tangy yellow bar on the room's opposite wall.**

FOLLOWING SPREAD **Grouped mirrors on a single expanse reflect a whole gallery of scenes. Using rows of circular mirrors inset on the wardrobe doors, I achieved that affect in the Hollywood Boulevard compound master bedroom.**

"I look at
my settings
through an
imaginary
viewfinder."

The Method Behind the Madness of Design

PROCESS

The course of a design project goes hand in hand with my creative process, but it has professional, chronological, technical, administrative, and economic procedures all its own. I could never substitute one for the other.

My way of seeing and transforming each job is intuitive and fluid. I don't say, "It's day one of the new job. What graphic element should I put on it?" or "Almost done. Let's wrap it up and go buy an unexpected door knocker." It's more conceptual and personal, both for me and for my clients. At the same time, there are specific phases that a project commences in and progresses through. So much time, so many individuals, and such specific circumstances shape every project.

Throughout a job, everyone involved has something to add, and there's always something to be learned from the various team members, in and out of the studio. Every client has an aesthetic, and I learn so much while discovering and articulating it with them. I'm also fortunate to work with some of the best vendors around. They are true artisans, expert collectors, and fellow designers who bring years of experience and insight to the total process. And without the KWID team, the most imaginative ideas would be left on the drawing board. They breathe so much spirit into every maneuver.

Maybe you want to hire a professional to design and decorate an interior but aren't sure what it involves. Or perhaps you need some loose directions for outlining a project you'll work on yourself. You might just be curious about the nuts and bolts of an interior design firm's operations. Check out my studio's process for a sense of our working style. It's not a definitive methodology—but it will give you some cues and mileposts to watch for as you proceed.

OVERLEAF **Trina Turk boutique, from start to finish: In the completed Palm Springs boutique, deluxe surfaces like mirrored tile, wet-look floor coverings, gleaming metallics, and Trina's vintage-inspired fashions transport shoppers back to the glory days of resorts like the Miami Beach Fontainebleau.**

OPPOSITE **Examining fabric options during the schematic design phase.**

Initial Concept Meeting

Everyone has what's referred to as a "program": a set of needs, conditions, and desires that will influence how I conceive of and execute the design.

In the initial concept conversation, my clients and I discuss their programs. Some are very forthright about their functional requirements: a hotel developer will want so many square feet for the restaurant, the gym, the standard guest rooms; the flow has to be as open as possible; the traditional hotel down the street appeals to an older clientele, while this hotel is for a younger business traveler; and so on. Many residential clients have a loose sense of their needs—for example, a comfortable but elegant family home—and some early ideas about style and color.

Since my job is to help clients push the visual envelope, I also discover more about their limits and temperaments for experimenting with their environment. The information that comes out of these early meetings will help me create the broad strokes in early design ideas, and possibly affect how we work in the future. I always ask early on if there are any spiritual needs, such as a desire to practice feng shui. It matters to some people intensely, while others don't follow it. For one job, we had to specially configure a staircase so that the number of levels harmonized with a feng shui principle of positive and negative steps.

Sheer shopping magic: I fabricated a room divider fabricated from chandelier crystals to create a glimmering veil between the showroom and fitting rooms in Trina's boutique.

Conceptual and Schematic Design

Feel, flow, and function guide the conceptual and schematic design phase. After the initial concept meeting, I pull together a variety of loose image presentations to illustrate some general design ideas for the project.

We use these pictorial presentations, mounted on large concept boards, to show a "wide shot" of a project's potential. One board could show a particular period influence, such as art deco; the second, a more traditional approach infused with color; a third might be a variation on or composite of the two. No two presentations are ever alike, because my interpretation of each client's program is always unique.

Obviously, the client's response to the presentation is key here. Some directions will be scrapped, and the vibe that feels the best will be reworked as color renderings that convey the idea of a room. We might also review some existing or historical images of a particular style—like a type of molding—and some color palettes during this phase. Once the direction is determined, we begin exploring architectural flows from space to space to help map out passages in an area, and adjacencies between architectural elements and furnishings, as well as preliminary elevations (computerized scale drawings of a facade) and sections (representations of a cross section that show how a room is put together).

We also ballpark budgets at this time, because these estimates will affect everything that comes next.

Where it all starts: these samples and accessories make up the design DNA that ultimately became Trina's retail flagship.

Design Development

Once I have a cohesive direction in mind, full-on transformation can begin. I start by reflecting on the concept to date, and refine my thinking about next steps. My staff and I then dive into modifying structural and architectural elements; rendering electrical plans and reflected ceiling plans; researching period and stylistic motifs; exploring functional options like kitchen and bath equipment; creating prototypes for custom designs and details, from furniture to floor coverings and fabric to fixtures; and shopping for essential design hallmarks such as paints, fabrics, and large specialty pieces around which a room will be designed.

There can be a fine line between schematic design and design development. The two phases are more like concentric circles than parallel lines, because we sometimes rethink or reconfigure a space when it isn't working or is too costly to implement. Without a doubt, the buzz kill happens during design development. Much of the time things are too expensive, and there's invariably an existing structural condition in a decades-old building with which we have to deal. That's why it's really crucial that the working drawings we generate are tight and accurate before construction begins. Time is money, and changes waste both.

During the design development phase, research, creativity, and cost-conscious "value engineering" all meet. KWID does a lot more legwork and research to find, say, a less expensive tile for two hundred hotel showers, or to work around a big area we discover once a wall is torn open, where all of the plumbing lines funnel down together. It takes what it takes timewise because we don't want to sacrifice the design integrity. Needless to say, there is a lot of budgetary fine-tuning throughout design development, including negotiating with contractors and consultants.

Palm Beach was a great resource for Trina's shop during design development. I soaked up its upper-crusty resort vibe, and found an array of furnishings, fixtures and accessories there for the boutique.

Implementation

Once we complete the design development on a project, we put a lot of miles on our cars.

During design implementation, a typical week might find me buzzing from the KWID bungalow to a job site under construction, then going to a vendor's workshop or supplier's showroom, and then stopping by boutiques, antique shops, flea markets, and thrift stores. A fabric that initially seemed perfect wasn't as fabulous as another one we found later, so it goes back; the molding that looks best isn't cost effective in quantity.

The larger design sources may sell to the trade at wholesale prices, but one-of-a-kind treasures can't be found at design centers. So I seek out unusual sources across the city and around the globe. I once tried to buy an amazing piece of tile and brass art that was in a bank. I called everyone, even spoke to the bank's president, but they wouldn't sell it to me. I've had better luck with other items; you just have to ask and you might get lucky. When we can, we take samples and pieces out "on memo," sort of like library books, to try them out in a space. Or I might take a digital photo of an amazing item that can't leave the store.

OPPOSITE **Life-size clothing dummies from the 1970s model clothing and hold back a curtain wall. I wanted them to be part of the architecture, not loose in the space.**

FOLLOWING SPREAD **Design modifies color and vice versa. If Trina's space wasn't daisy yellow, it might not convey a resort feel, and all white would be too predictable.**

As glamorous as it seems, this "trying-on" period always boils down to being certain. I want to be accommodating to my clients' needs, so I want to show them a tangible example of something. It actually saves a lot of time, and lets us value engineer with quality in mind as much as price.

"Seeing and transforming each job is intuitive and fluid."

KWID
EXCLUSIVES

Regardless of the retail and wholesale resources available, sometimes I just can't find what I have in my mind's eye (or what the client's budget allows).

So instead of settling for less than the perfect size, look, or price, I sit down and create it myself.

With hotel projects especially, there are very specific needs that our work has to accommodate. They can include architectural relationships (such as size and scale), hospitality factors (like a minibar and TV storage), and durability requests (no raw silk, please). My boutique hotel designs also require anomalies that make the guest experience at that property completely one of a kind. They help shape the hotel's individual brand and identity, and are never the assembly-line replications you'll find in impersonal chain hotels. The idea of "economies of scale" can apply as much to yardage run for a two-hundred-room resort as it can to two hundred properties nationwide.

Many residential and commercial clients also understand the value in making something unique to their own space. Obviously, custom fabrication varies in cost. It may involve having a high-quality piece made rather than buying it retail—or it may require the pricey manufacture of a mold, custom milling of fabric or carpet, special glazes, finishes, or trims, and so on. But to optimize space, assure quality, dial in a vibe, and make something unexpected, it's worth the research and effort. If you aren't in the position to commission work, be resourceful. With a carpenter's help, you could build your own design.

Although mass production doesn't always compromise the integrity of a design, there really isn't a lot of interesting stuff out there to buy. We looked high and low for barstools for Maison 140 but ended up going with my own design because everything else was "too-too." Above the mantels in the Estrella suites, I hand-painted abstract frescoes to conserve dwindling funds. Even if affordable, great-quality products were available all over, I'd still keep designing in every medium. It's fun and it keeps my brain moving. In the not-too-distant future, I'd love for everyone to be able to add a KWID design to his or her life.

I rarely find fabric, carpet, furnishings, and accessories that all meet my specific color, scale, and yardage needs. So I make them for the job at hand.

OVERLEAF **Casper wingback chaise, designed for Viceroy.**

OPPOSITE **Cameo carpet, designed for Viceroy.**

FOLLOWING SPREAD

LEFT: **Spyros fabric, designed for Estrella.** RIGHT: **Griffin wallpaper, designed for Viceroy.**

OPPOSITE

TOP RIGHT: **Midnight Lace ladderback chair, designed for Viceroy.** BOTTOM RIGHT: **Dorset armchair, designed for Viceroy.**
TOP LEFT: **Porfirio armchair, designed for Viceroy.**
BOTTOM LEFT: **Casper wing chair, designed for Viceroy.**

ABOVE **Captain Kidd chair, designed for Whist.**

OPPOSITE **Drysdale sofa, designed for Viceroy.**

BELOW **Madame Butterfly headboard, designed for Maison 140.**

"Instead of settling for less than perfect, I create something special."

Styling My Future

EVOLUTION

258

Will the day arrive when the unanticipated becomes predictable, simple gestures cease to visually surprise, and KWID's dramatic expression loses its sense of humor?

It's a tough question but an inevitable one. The answer must always be a bold "No!" The nature of design itself is a process. It doesn't just end with the last stroke, the final nail, the hundredth stitch, or the closing invoice. Since there is always potential for change, there is always the possibility for sophisticated spontaneity and the elegance of the unexpected.

As much as I dislike putting limits on myself, my sole aspiration for KWID is to grow broader, not bigger. I want my company to always be able to maintain its boutique approach and the level of design integrity that it's known for. I see my creative development lying in projects that challenge me to explore, integrate, and elevate diversely historical architectural settings.

Though many jobs provide designers with great opportunities to reveal a property's history, those projects often lack biographical significance. They may be nicely updated, retain architectural integrity, and evoke emotion, but don't feel touched by the individuals who designed and lived in them. They've been remodeled, but they haven't evolved. Infused with both heritage and innovation, KWID's Trousdale Place engagement is a special example of evolution in action: it reflects appreciation for what's historic, courage to try something new, the interplay of staged and real life, the importance of collaboration between client and consultant, and even my own evolution from fledgling set decorator to established interior designer.

Magnificent obsession: the Trousdale Place estate was originally designed in 1965 by famed Beverly Hills architect Harold Levitt for film producer Ross Hunter. The driving force behind Hollywood classics like *Airport* and *Pillow Talk*, Hunter was actively involved in every stage of design. I retained many details original to the house, including terrazzo floors, the lattice canopy over the patio (reportedly Hunter's suggestion), and opulent lion's head door handles.

Like an enticing trailer for a blockbuster movie, these ornately carved, 22-karat gold door handles hint at the elongated scale, sumptuous detailing, and dramatic vignettes awaiting inside.

OPPOSITE A reading nook overlooking the swimming pool melds the simplest hallmarks of Southern California living with the fanciest old world artifacts (a Napoleon-style console, an Asian bust sculpted from red limestone, a formal pair of alabaster table lamps).

Gold standard: Ross Hunter used yellow hues and citrus-themed artwork throughout the original house. The walls in the master bedroom (opposite) are covered in grass cloth with a gold-leaf backing; the carpet and upholstery glow in coordinating shades.

ABOVE In an adjacent room, modern armchairs upholstered in daisy silk set off a nineteenth-century French demi-lune table and a carved stairway banister imported from Spain.

LEFT A field of shimmering ceramics in the kitchen adorn silver-backed grass-cloth walls.

Lofty drama: Stratospheric ceilings inspired the addition of towering cabinets that provide practical storage and aesthetic interest. In the library, the KWID-designed pagoda cabinet (left) is coated in a gold leaf and metallic alloy. An eighteenth-century French vitrine (above) finished in an antique persimmon hue provides a similarly statuesque focal point in the living room.

"There is always the possibility for sophisticated spontaneity and the elegance of the unexpected."

270

OVERLEAF **In both its original and re-created incarnations, the Trousdale Place estate holds fast to Ross Hunter's personal belief that "the way life looks in my pictures is the way I want life to be." I made the transition from stage to interior design for very similar reasons.**

ABOVE AND RIGHT **All that heaven allows: With floor-to-ceiling glass to the east, gold silk walls to the north and south, and a vintage Lalique chandelier halo, the dining room floats high above Beverly Hills. The armchairs were reupholstered in spearmint silk, and the table was restained and polished. Underfoot, glossy refinished parquet floors and new wool shag ground the space with organic, modern textures.**

LEFT **The property's screening room underwent a digital makeover yet maintained many of its original decorative hallmarks: an eleven-foot sofa tailored to the room's dimensions was re-covered in a bouclé fabric, and Hunter's modern armchairs were updated in a sleek cotton blend. New furnishings included a pair of consoles from the 1940s and a dramatic pewter coffee table crafted in the 1970s by a French sculptor.**

ABOVE **In the media room, a set of chairs designed by Billy Haines were refinished and re-covered in a loosely woven linen, then paired with one of the estate's card tables.**

274

Re-creating a property with such a distinguished background was a fabulous challenge. The backbone of the project was Hal Levitt's spectacular design, which was thoughtfully sited and artfully built. Other homes of his in the area have been remodeled so extensively that their original intention and integrity disappear. I wanted to do the Trousdale Place estate justice.

The heart of the house lay in its collection of furnishings and accessories hand-picked by the original owner. Deciding which elements to restore and which to revise required appreciation for history without slavish devotion to it, and a sensitivity to my clients' needs and the collections they wanted to integrate into the design. While the existing house had a stately vintage glamour, it lacked contemporary intensity. In the redesign process, I rediscovered how to mix eras, experiences, and media, so that the rooms and grounds found the energy that characterizes modern glamour. It's a notion guided by emotion and intuition, not an unwavering set of design rules.

At its core, KWID will always be a design firm that envisions and realizes aspects of the art of living. So I have to personally keep exploring what turns me on, through traveling, reading, and general day-to-day learning. Over time, I see myself doing different types of architectural design projects in far-flung locations, and building the KWID product design line for every need and budget. And I hope my own creative envelope is continually pushed into new stylistic directions by my clients' requests. Being open to knowledge is key, because good results can always come of it.

A grand gilt mirror reflects an unexpectedly fresh formality on the main terrace, a space visible from nearly every room in the house. Juxtaposed with the ornate Brown Jordan patio furniture, the whole setting is at once composed and capricious.

As my business and I both grow, the challenges will be more than simply designing, say, a great cabinet handle. But that won't stop me from making that one small piece the most glamorous thing in the room.

Palatial horizon: A view of the swimming pool canopy from a living room chaise longue mirrors the grandeur and formal comfort that permeate the entire estate.

Fabrics, Wallcoverings, and Trims

Astek Wallcoverings
15933 Arminta Street
Van Nuys, CA 91406
818.901.9876
www.astekwallcovering.com
The most fabulous new and vintage papers

Bergamo Fabrics
7 West 22nd Street, 2nd Floor
New York, NY 10010
212.462.1010
and in other national showrooms
www.bergamofabrics.com
Amazing colors and textural fabrics

Clarence House
8687 Melrose Avenue, B504
Los Angeles, CA 90069
310.652.0200
and in other national and international
showrooms
www.clarencehousefabrics.com
*When you need that perfect color in a
thousand different hands, it's here*

Embroidery Palace
464 South Robertson Boulevard
Los Angeles, CA 90048
310.273.8003
Beautiful custom embellishments

Houlès
8584 Melrose Avenue
Los Angeles, CA 90069
310.652.6171
and in other national and international
showrooms
www.houles.com
*The best bejeweling accessories for fabrics—
and whatever else comes to mind*

Keith H. McCoy & Associates
8710 Melrose Avenue
Los Angeles, CA 90069
310.657.7150
Groovy prints in a vintage kind of way

Pratt & Lambert Paints
P.O. Box 22
Buffalo, NY 14240
800.289.7728
and through national retail locations
www.prattandlambert.com
Fine paint in the most wonderful colors

F. Schumacher Company
79 Madison Avenue
New York, NY 10016
212.213.7900
and in other national and international
showrooms
www.fschumacher.com
*Incredible selection of fine fabrics,
carpets, and wallpapers*

West Coast Trimmings
466 South Robertson Boulevard
Los Angeles, CA 90048
323.272.6569
*A small, service-oriented trim shop special-
izing in vintage and custom everything*

Finishes, Hardware, and Fixtures

Accent Hardware
2433 Main Street,
Santa Monica, CA 90405
310.392.6292
*Where service reigns—a must when
specifying hardware and fixtures*

Cane & Basket Supply Co.
1283 South Cochran Avenue
Los Angeles, CA 90019
323.939.9644
www.caneandbasket.com
*Natural weaving and decorative materials,
from bamboo poles to cane webbing*

Crown City Hardware
1047 North Allen Avenue
Pasadena, CA 91104
626.794.1188
www.crowncityhardware.com
*If you're in need of hardware or any
miscellaneous fitting*

Dornbracht USA
1700 Executive Drive S, Ste. 600
Duluth, GA 30096
800.774.1181
and in other international showrooms
www.dornbracht.com
*For a clean modern look that won't compete
with other design elements*

Faneuil Furniture Hardware
163 Main Street
Salem, NH 03079
603.898.7733
*A great collection of cool and unusual old-
school hardware*

Koontz Hardware
8914 Santa Monica Boulevard
West Hollywood, CA 90069
310.652.0123
www.koontz.com
I'm always surprised by what I come across here, from great hardware to brass beads

Liz's Antique Hardware
453 South La Brea Avenue
Los Angeles, CA 90036
323.939.4403
www.lahardware.com
An all-time favorite—hands down the best antique hardware store in Los Angeles

Rhomboid Sax
8904 Beverly Boulevard
West Hollywood, CA 90048
310.550.0170
Stellar bathroom paraphernalia and prompt customer service

Superior Moulding
5953 Sepulveda Boulevard
Van Nuys, CA 91411
818.376.1415
From moldings to medallions

Van Dyke's Restorers catalog
P.O. Box 278
39771 S.D. Highway 34
Woonsocket, SD 57385
800.558.1234
www.vandykes.com
A catalog for your inner furniture lover

Waterworks
70 Backus Avenue
Danbury, CT 06810
800.927.2120
and in other national retail locations
www.waterworks.com
For a classic fit

Furniture and Accessories

J. F. Chen
8414 Melrose Avenue
West Hollywood, CA 90069
323.655.6310
Exquisitely unique selection of vintage and mid-century-modern Asian, European, and American furniture, accessories, and art

Coconut Company
131 Greene Street
New York, NY 10012
212.539.1940
A store that gets it, from Empire to '80s modern

Downtown
719 North La Cienega Boulevard
Los Angeles, CA 90069
310.652.7461
Furniture, lighting, and accessories that will make any room sing

Eat My Handbag Bitch
6 Dray Walk, The Old Truman Brewery
91-95 Brick Lane
London E1 6QL
020.7375.3100
www.eatmyhandbagbitch.co.uk
An unbelievable collection of modern furniture and accoutrements

Gearys of Beverly Hills
351 North Beverly Drive
Beverly Hills, CA 90210
800.793.6670
www.gearys.com
Lavish tabletop accessories, stemware, and linens—and impeccable service to match

Harris Kratz Antiques
3611 South Dixie Highway
West Palm Beach, FL 33405
561.832.9062
Fabulous—truly exquisite finds

Kenneth Lynch & Sons
The Book of Garden Ornaments catalog
84 Danbury Road
P.O. Box 488
Wilton, CT 06897-0488
203.762.8363
www.klynchandsons.com
Whatever you want for gardens

Marché Paul Bert
Paris Saint-Ouen Flea Market
18 Rue Paul Bert
93400 Saint-Ouen
France
Seven charming aisles of stands that sell everything from dishware to dining tables—just don't go in the winter

Overdose on Design
182 Brick Lane
London E1 6SA
0171.613.1266
www.overdoseondesign.com
The modern furniture lover's paradise

Residence
4464 West Adams Boulevard
Los Angeles, CA 90016
323.731.9991
The best upholsterers

Rubbish
1630 Silverlake Boulevard
Los Angeles, CA 90026
323.661.5575
An old-time favorite where I always load up on great finds

Sticks & Stones Floral Design Studio
636A North Almont Drive
West Hollywood, CA 90069
310.385.8616
For an unexpected floral flourish

Sunview
1325 South La Brea Avenue
Los Angeles, CA 90019
323.954. 9263
Amazing furniture and finishes

Alfie's Antique Market
13-25 Church Street
London NW8 8DT
020.7723.6066
The antique mall that never ends—a huge place with an amazing bag of tricks

Books and Printed Reference Materials

Hennessey+Ingalls
214 Wilshire Boulevard
Santa Monica, CA 90401
310.458.9074
www.hennesseyingalls.com
*America's best visual arts bookseller, from
its colossal inventory, to its knowledgeable
staff, to its Morphosis-designed storefront*

Powell's City of Books
1005 West Burnside
Portland, OR 97209
503. 228. 4651
*Largest independent bookstore—new
and used*

Zwemmer
Design & Architecture Shop
72 Charing Cross Road
London WC2H 0BE
020.7240.1559
Media & Contemporary Art Shop
80 Charing Cross Road
London WC2H 9BH
020.7240.4157
www.zwemmer.com
*An unbelievably vast selection of new and
vintage arts publications, available in the
company's specialty stores, museum, and
gallery shops all over the U.K.*

Linens and Loungewear

Anichini
466 North Robertson Boulevard
Los Angeles, CA 90048
310.657.4292
and in other national retail locations
www.anichini.com
*Old-world craftsmanship, unexpected colors,
unstinting detail, and a custom approach*

Frette
449 North Rodeo Drive
Beverly Hills, CA 90210
310.273.8540
and in other national and international retail
locations
www.frette.it
*A glamorous favorite offering ultra-sleek cot-
ton, linen, silk, and cashmere*

Hermès
24, Rue du Faubourg Saint-Honoré
Paris 75008
01.40.17.47.17
and in other national and international retail
locations
*The legendary Paris boutique is the place
for the chicest blankets and table linens in
sumptuous textures and colors*

Pratesi
9024 Burton Way
Beverly Hills, CA 90211
310.274.7661
and in other national and international retail
locations
www.pratesi.com
*The most sensual cashmere throws in hot
colors*

Crating and Shipping

Hedley's Humpers
Units 1/2/3/4
3 St. Leonard's Road
London NW10 6F5
0181.965.8733
and locations in New York, Paris,
and Antibes
www.hedleyshumpers.com
Expensive but worth every shilling

Padded Wagon
163 Exterior Street,
Bronnx, NY 10451
212.222.4880
www.padded.com
and other national locations
*Trustworthy packing, crating, shipping, and
storage at home and abroad–they're
"movers, not shakers"*

Plycon Van Lines
4240 West 190th Street, Suite C
Torrance, CA 90504
310.419.1200
and locations in New York, Florida, Illinois,
Texas, Maryland and Georgia
www.plyconvanlines.com
*My choice for coast-to-coast fine furniture
transport in the United States*